P9-CQH-345

THE JOSSEY-BASS NONPROFIT & PUBLIC MANAGEMENT SERIES ALSO INCLUDES:

Creating Your Employee Handbook

A DO-IT-YOURSELF KIT FOR NONPROFITS

MANAGEMENT **M** CENTER

Leyna Bernstein, author

Jossey-Bass Publishers
San Francisco

Jossey-Bass books and products are available through most bookstores. To contact Jossey-Bass directly, call (888) 378-2537, fax to (800) 605-2665, or visit our website at www.josseybass.com.

Substantial discounts on bulk quantities of Jossey-Bass books are available to corporations, professional associations, and other organizations. For details and discount information, contact the special sales department at Jossey-Bass.

This book is printed on paper containing a minimum of 10 percent postconsumer waste and manufactured in the United States of America.

Interior design by Carolyn Deacy

Library of Congress Cataloging-in-Publication Data

Bernstein, Leyna.
   Creating your employee handbook : a do-it-yourself kit for nonprofits / by Leyna Bernstein.—1st ed.
      p. cm.—(The Jossey-Bass nonprofit and public management series)
Includes bibliographical references and index.
   ISBN 0-7879-4844-6 (pbk. : acid-free paper)
 1. Employee handbooks. 2. Nonprofit organizations—Personnel management—Handbooks, manuals, etc. I. Title. II. Series.
   HF5549.5.E423 B473 2000
   658.4'55—dc21

                                99-006892

PB Printing   10 9 8 7 6 5 4 3 2 1   FIRST EDITION

The Jossey-Bass Nonprofit and
Public Management Series

Acknowledgments

This book could not have been created without the suggestions and sample policies provided by The Management Center's nonprofit clients. In particular, we would like to thank the following organizations for lending us copies of their own employee handbooks:

Affordable Housing Associates

Alzheimer's Association, Bay Area

The American Red Cross

Battered Women's Alternatives

Big Brothers/Big Sisters of the East Bay, Inc.

California Association of Local Arts Agencies

California Chamber of Commerce

The Family Violence Prevention Fund

Golden Gate Community, Inc.

Mid-Peninsula Management Corporation

The NAMES Project

SeniorNet

The Women's Philharmonic

CREDITS

This book has been made possible by grants from The David and Lucile Packard Foundation and The James Irvine Foundation.

PUBLISHERS

Jossey-Bass Publishers

The Management Center,

Robert Walker,
Executive director

Leyna Bernstein, Author

Baillee Serbin, National editor

Contents

Preface

In our work with nonprofits, the consulting staff of The Management Center often receives requests for assistance in crafting and communicating personnel policies. *Creating Your Employee Handbook: A Do-It-Yourself Kit for Nonprofits* is one way in which we are responding to this need in the nonprofit community.

Creating Your Employee Handbook is designed to be a practical tool to use once you are ready to write or update your handbook. You can use this book as a step-by-step guide for creating your own handbook or use specific sections to update existing policies and identify new ones. We hope that you will also use this handbook to gain insight into why certain policies are needed in your organization and which don't fit. We also hope that this book will broaden your knowledge of personnel practices in the nonprofit sector.

Creating Your Employee Handbook demonstrates how policies can be written to reflect your organization's size, mission, and work culture. Most policies are offered in three versions to illustrate how policies can be customized. In the world of employee handbooks, one size does not fit all. We caution you not to use language taken directly from handbooks from other sources (including this book) without first ensuring that the policies and wording reflect your organizational reality. It is especially important for you to include only policies and practices that your organization can implement fully and consistently.

Creating Your Employee Handbook is divided into five parts: "Starting Your Handbook Off Right," "Presenting Clear Employment and Employee Development Policies," "Creating Well-Crafted Benefits Policies," "Developing Fair, Straightforward Policies for Workplace

Standards and Practices," and "Clarifying End-of-Employment Policies." Each part covers a broad spectrum of personnel policies, most presented in three versions. Although the order and format of policy presentation is designed to guide you through the creation of your own employee handbook, do not assume that all of the policies presented need be included in your handbook. We offer as complete a collection of policies as possible so that you can select those that best fit your organization's current needs. It is the rare organization that would include every single policy contained in this book in its employee handbook.

This is the first national edition of *Creating Your Employee Handbook*. We expect to update and expand this handbook continually as we work with our clients and gain additional knowledge about the personnel policy needs of nonprofits. We hope to hear from you about your experience using this book. We have included a feedback sheet at the back of the book for your comments and suggestions.

San Francisco, California   Leyna Bernstein
September 1999

About The Management Center

THE MANAGEMENT CENTER is a leading resource for nonprofit management support in Northern California. Since 1977, we've been helping good causes manage better. Our mission is to help nonprofit organizations achieve their full potential; through effective consulting, training, and information resources, we assist nonprofit leaders in strengthening their organizations and enhancing their community service. Our various activities include:

- Board and organizational development
- Human resources management
- Programs for nonprofit leaders
- Recognizing and promoting excellence

For more information, please don't hesitate to contact us at:

The Management Center
870 Market Street, Suite 800
San Francisco, CA 94102-2903
Voice: (415) 362-9735
Fax: (415) 362-4603
E-mail: tmc@tmcenter.org
Internet: http://www.tmcenter.org

About the Author

LEYNA BERNSTEIN is a writer, consultant, and trainer with expertise in organizational development and human resources management. She is a principal with Bernstein & Associates in San Francisco and serves as affiliate consultant in human resources with The Management Center.

Through her consulting practice, Bernstein has provided human resources consulting and training services to organizations since 1993 and now works exclusively with the nonprofit sector. Prior to founding her own firm, she spent over a decade as a human resources executive with some of the San Francisco Bay Area's leading socially responsible companies.

Bernstein has a long history of active involvement with the nonprofit community. She is a member of the board of the San Francisco Jewish Film Festival and chairs its personnel committee; she also serves as vice president for planning on the board of The Women's Philharmonic.

Bernstein is the author of *Best Practices: The Model Employee Handbook for California Nonprofits* (Jossey-Bass, 1998). In 1997, Bernstein and her husband, Peter Barnes, founded Mesa Refuge, a nonprofit writer's retreat in Point Reyes Station, California.

She lives in San Francisco and Point Reyes Station with her husband and two sons.

Introduction

HOW AN EFFECTIVE EMPLOYEE HANDBOOK CAN IMPROVE YOUR ORGANIZATION

Most of us tend to think of an employee handbook as a dry, rather boring document written in legalese. Although your handbook is a legal document that can help protect your organization from employment litigation by clearly spelling out organizational policies, there are many other reasons to provide a handbook to each of your employees.

An employee handbook is not the same thing as a compendium of every policy your organization uses in its operations. An employee handbook is a communication tool for you to use with your employees. Your employee handbook should contain the policies and information your employees need to guide them on a day-to-day basis.

Your employee handbook has the potential to be a powerful tool for communicating and emphasizing organizational values and the benefits of employment with you. Most new employees start work carrying a large package of assumptions about their new work environment. This is especially true of employees who are new to the nonprofit sector. Because the work of nonprofits is so strongly mission-based, many new employees arrive with expectations of an idealized work environment. These expectations can differ widely from the reality of your organization's work culture and practices.

Use your employee handbook to communicate clearly the kind of workplace you offer: not only policies and procedures but also the "personality" and values unique to your organization. The tone in which the book is written, the specific language used in the book, and even the typeface are all factors that communicate information about what kind of organization you are.

Use the information in your employee handbook to establish job performance expectations and to set the stage for the kind of behaviors you want to promote in the work environment. Your employee handbook should also be an integral part of your orientation program for new employees. Be sure to give new employees the opportunity to read the handbook, and set aside time for their questions about its content.

Include copies of job descriptions, performance evaluations, and frequently used personnel forms in each handbook so that you create opportunities for your employees to use the handbook throughout their employment. (Compiling your handbook in a binder format allows for the inclusion of forms and other documents.)

Think of your employee handbook as an internal marketing and communication tool. Much as brochures, newsletters, and annual reports help your organization present a message to donors and others in the community you serve, an effectively written handbook helps you communicate with your employees.

Every handbook should have an acknowledgment form for the employee to return and sign. The form should indicate that the employee has read the handbook and understands the policies it contains (see the sample in Resource C). The acknowledgment form is also the means by which you reinforce at-will employment status (if you are an at-will employer). Be certain that every new employee signs such an acknowledgment and that the signed acknowledgment is placed in his or her personnel file.

There is no one perfect way to write an employee handbook. However, too many handbooks get read once and then languish in a desk drawer. You may never create a "bestseller," but my hope is that this book will help you create the best possible handbook for your nonprofit organization.

HOW TO USE THIS HANDBOOK

AS A TEMPLATE

This handbook is designed to be used as a template or guide for creating your own nonprofit personnel policy handbook. The order in which the policies are presented is logical but somewhat arbitrary. Certainly there is no one right way to produce an employee handbook, and you should modify, delete, or rearrange policies to suit your needs.

TO UPDATE EXISTING POLICIES

Scan this book for policies that are missing from your own. Pay particular attention to policies that are marked with this symbol:

It means that the policy is required by or related to a state or federal labor law. You will find state-by-state listings of specific statutes that mandate personnel policies in the Resources section of this book.

TO ENHANCE EXISTING POLICIES

Even if your own employee handbook is up-to-date, you can find ideas here for improving communication of information, adding innovative practices, and rearranging the format of your handbook. Look for this symbol:

It indicates innovative policies.

Inside the back cover of the book is a computer disk (see "How to Use This Disk" on the final page). On the disk, you will find text files of all the policies in *Creating Your Employee Handbook*. You may use, edit, copy, and distribute these policies within your organization, as long as all copyright and credit information remains intact. Any further distribution, in print or electronic form, is strictly prohibited.

SUGGESTIONS ABOUT FORMAT

- Distribute your handbook in a three-ring binder so that you can add and delete pages without needing to reprint the entire document.

- Date each page in your handbook so that you can identify the latest version or determine when a policy was updated, changed, or added. Retain copies of old policies for your records.

- Make your handbook graphically interesting by using icons, different typefaces, and boldfaced type. Include plenty of white space; handbooks that contain page after page of small type are difficult to read.

- Provide samples of frequently used personnel forms, such as the employee's job description, your performance evaluation, and change of status and corrective action forms.

- At the back of the handbook, include an acknowledgment form to be signed, dated, and returned by the employee and placed in his or her personnel file. The acknowledgment form should indicate that the employee has read the handbook.

- Create an index in addition to your table of contents to help employees find a policy based on key words, even if they don't know its formal name.

ABOUT SAMPLE POLICIES

Most of the sample policies in this handbook are offered in three versions: the Creative Approach, primarily for small or informal organizations; the By-the-Book Approach, for mid-sized or traditional agencies; and the Leading-Edge Approach, for large or progressive institutions. By offering three versions of most policies, we can show that *how* a policy is written, in addition to its intent, reflects organizational culture.

Fewer versions are provided under the following circumstances:

- If certain sample policies apply equally to two or all three approaches. This happens when a policy is either very short or dictated in detail by federal law.

- If policies don't apply to or aren't legally required in smaller organizations, which are represented by the Creative and By-the-Book Approaches. Other policies are simply not formally stated in smaller organizations, even though an informal version of the policy may exist in practice.

- If policies are especially innovative or expensive or if they provide complex optional benefits, in which case they are offered only in the Leading-Edge version. Leading-Edge Approach samples are written from the perspective of a large organization.

Although the three versions are written to reflect different workplace styles, we encourage you to read all three policy versions and to select policies from any of them, depending on which best suits your needs. Never put a new policy into place without being sure that you can follow through on it consistently. Many organizations get into trouble by publishing policies they cannot support due to time, budget, or staffing constraints.

CREATIVE APPROACH

The Creative Approach version is written for nonprofits with a staff of no more than twenty employees and an informal work environment. Such a small, informal organization would typically need only a small number of formal personnel policies. Most often the executive director manages personnel policies and human resources practices in organizations of this type.

BY-THE-BOOK APPROACH

The By-the-Book Approach version is written for medium-sized nonprofits that have twenty to one hundred employees and hence a more structured work environment. An organization with this more conservative type of work culture would implement all legally required and commonly followed personnel policies but might not offer more unique or cutting-edge policies. A director of operations or the office manager frequently manages personnel policies and human resources practices in this type of organization.

LEADING-EDGE APPROACH

The Leading-Edge Approach version is written for nonprofits with more than one hundred employees and an innovative and progressive work environment. An organization of this size, with a tendency toward experimentation, would implement all conventional personnel policies and many less common policies as well. A director of human resources usually manages personnel policies and human resources practices in an organization of this size. Human resources assistance to employees is generally provided by the director of human resources and an HR staff.

A WORD OR TWO
ABOUT THE LAW

It is essential that you have your own handbook reviewed by a qualified employment attorney before it is printed and distributed. Many of the policies contained in this handbook address complex legal issues, and the only way to be certain that you are adequately covering your specific obligations is to consult with your own legal counsel.

Your goal should be to satisfy your organization's risk management needs while providing a set of sensible, humane workplace policies.

PART ONE

Starting Your Handbook Off Right

CHAPTER ONE

Policies for a Good First Impression

WELCOME

▶ CREATIVE APPROACH

Welcome to Creative Agency. We believe that outstanding people are the key to our success. Through the efforts of our staff members, Creative Agency has established itself as a leading organization in our community. To ensure our continued success, we feel it is important that all staff members understand our policies and procedures. This handbook is intended to help familiarize you with them. We encourage you to use this handbook as a valuable resource for understanding our organization.

If you have any questions, please do not hesitate to ask either your manager or any member of our management team.

My best wishes to you, and thank you for taking this first step in getting to know Creative Agency.

Sincerely,

Alison Barnsely, Executive Director

▶ BY-THE-BOOK APPROACH

Welcome. It is our pleasure to welcome you as a member of the staff of By-the-Book Agency. You are an integral part of a dynamic nonprofit organization.

As an employee of By-the-Book Agency, you are a community relations representative both on and off the job. We ask that you learn about our organization so that you can speak confidently about By-the-Book in all your associations.

We designed this manual to help you understand what your benefits are and what policies guide your day-to-day activities here at By-the-Book.

We think working with By-the-Book is a special opportunity. We hope that you will find your employment a matter of both pride and satisfaction and that it will be mutually productive and enjoyable.

Sincerely,

Vernon Lee, Executive Director

Jennifer Nelson, Board President

CONSIDER THIS

Begin your handbook with a statement of welcome signed by the executive director and perhaps the board chair. The first few pages that an employee sees should be a positive reflection of your organization's culture and values.

Do *not* start your handbook with a statement about at-will employment! You do not want employees' first impressions to be set with information about termination. There are several opportunities to protect yourself legally in the text of the handbook.

Include some information about your organization—preferably a mission statement and some organizational history as well.

▶ LEADING-EDGE APPROACH

Welcome! Leading-Edge Agency is a special organization made up of people who work together to affirm our connection to humanity and to serve the community we all share. We strive to operate in a work environment that is marked by honest, responsible, and sincere human interaction. As a team, our aim is to support each other in achieving individual and organizational goals.

This handbook serves as a guide for working together. Further, it outlines Leading-Edge's commitments to our employees and the commitments we expect in return. Please read it carefully and use it as you need. If we live our shared values daily and if we follow these stated guidelines, we will all enjoy an exceptional working environment.

Sincerely,

Wendy K. Shannon, Executive Director

Claudia Albano, H.R. Director

EQUAL EMPLOYMENT OPPORTUNITY

▶ CREATIVE APPROACH

We maintain a strong policy of equal employment opportunity. We seek to achieve equal opportunity for all staff members as articulated by federal, state, and local laws. Creative Agency actively seeks to recruit individuals without regard to race, creed, color, disability, marital status, veteran status, national origin, age, or physical handicap. Our equal employment opportunity philosophy applies to all aspects of employment, including recruitment, training, promotion, transfer, job benefits, pay, and dismissal.

▶ BY-THE-BOOK APPROACH

It is the policy of this agency to afford equal opportunity in all aspects of employment to all persons without discrimination on the basis of race, religion, sex, national origin, ethnicity, age, physical disabilities, political affiliation, color, marital status, or medical condition. This policy shall apply to all employees, applicants for employment, board and committee members, and volunteers and extends to all phases of employment, including recruitment, screening, referral, hiring, training, promotion, discharge or lay-off, rehiring, compensation, and benefits.

▶ LEADING-EDGE APPROACH

WORKPLACE DIVERSITY

We cultivate a work environment that encourages fairness, teamwork, and respect among all employees. We are firmly committed to maintaining a work atmosphere in which people of diverse backgrounds and lifestyles may grow personally and professionally.

EQUAL EMPLOYMENT OPPORTUNITY

Leading-Edge Agency is an equal opportunity employer. It is our strong belief that equal opportunity for all employees is central to

CONSIDER THIS

By putting these policies at the beginning of your handbook, you are emphasizing the importance you place on creating a fair, respectful, and discrimination-free work environment.

In writing your EEO policy, be aware that the law does allow you to exclude a certain protected group if you can prove that the exclusion is based on a "bona fide occupational qualification (BFOQ)." For example, if your organization runs a residential shelter for battered women, you may be able to exclude men from the position of live-in coordinator.

If you have questions about this or other hiring issues, it's a good idea to speak with an employment attorney to identify your options in each particular situation.

the continuing success of our organization. We will not discriminate against an employee or applicant for employment because of
race, religion, sex, national origin, ethnicity, age, physical disabilities, political affiliation, sexual orientation, color, gender identity
characteristics or expression, marital status, veteran status, or medical condition (for example, AIDS, AIDS-related condition, or cancer) in hiring, promotion, demotion, training, benefits, transfers,
layoffs, terminations, recommendations, rates of pay, or other
forms of compensation. Opportunity is provided to all employees
on the basis of qualifications and job requirements.

AFFIRMATIVE ACTION

▶ **CREATIVE APPROACH**

(not applicable: no requirement)

▶ **BY-THE-BOOK APPROACH**

(not applicable: no requirement)

▶ **LEADING-EDGE APPROACH**

In support of our commitment to equal opportunity in all matters relating to employment without regard to race, color, religion, disability, sex, veteran status, marital status, age, or national origin, we maintain a positive, continuing program of affirmative action.

We strive to achieve and maintain a diverse workforce. Toward that end, we undertake the following actions, which represent some but not all of our affirmative action efforts:

1. Fair and consistent hiring, promotion, and salary administration practices that comply with our equal opportunity policy

2. Communication about our equal employment opportunity policy to all employees on a regular basis

3. Training for all supervisory employees on ways to support and develop a diverse workforce

4. Regular reports to the board of directors on all activities and procedures designed to implement our policy of equal employment opportunity

5. Implementation of focused recruitment strategies when and if our staff does not meet our diversity goals

CONSIDER THIS

All employers are responsible for ensuring equal employment opportunity in their organizations and for abiding by state and federal civil rights laws.

Whether or not you adopt a formal affirmative action policy depends on the size of your organization and the terms of any contracts you may have with governmental organizations.

An affirmative action plan is generally much more detailed than an EEO policy and includes specific actions and strategies for recruiting, developing, promoting, and retaining a diverse workforce. AA plans are usually developed and reviewed by an employment attorney. Any affirmative action plan must be backed up by the internal capacity and resources to implement it consistently. Your organization can be held accountable for noncompliance even if what you do or don't do is not, strictly speaking, illegal.

AMERICANS WITH DISABILITIES ACT (ADA)

CONSIDER THIS

CONSIDER THIS

If you have fifty or more employees, you are required to comply with the ADA. Having a written ADA policy is a good first step, but ADA compliance requires that you put into practice specific procedures to ensure that you are not placing unnecessary barriers to employment before individuals with disabilities.

To comply fully with the ADA, an employer must identify the essential functions of each distinct job in the organization and be prepared to offer reasonable accommodations to allow a disabled applicant or employee access to the job.

The workplace must also be physically accessible, or the employer must be willing to make reasonable accommodations to the workplace (not to the extent of creating a financial hardship for the employer) to allow a person with disabilities to function in the job.

▶ CREATIVE APPROACH

(not legally required in organizations with fifty or fewer employees)

▶ BY-THE-BOOK APPROACH

(see Leading-Edge Approach; policy is dictated by federal law)

▶ LEADING-EDGE APPROACH

Leading-Edge Agency welcomes applications from people with disabilities. We fully support the Americans with Disabilities Act of 1990. We have taken steps to make our work facilities barrier-free and accessible as defined by state and federal statutes.

We have sought to identify the essential functions and physical requirements of all distinct jobs at Leading-Edge and will make reasonable accommodations through scheduling, task reassignment, and other methods to accommodate applicants and employees with disabilities.

HANDBOOK USE AND PURPOSE

▶ CREATIVE APPROACH

The purpose of this staff member handbook is to outline certain information about your employment with Creative Agency. The policies described here are in effect and supersede all other versions of these policies previously given to you either orally or in writing.

The provisions of these policies may, at the discretion of our board of directors, be modified, revoked, or changed from time to time. Also note that our policies do not cover every situation that can and will arise in the workplace. Above all, we ask that you exercise common courtesy and common sense while on the job.

If you have questions regarding your employment or anything contained in these policies, please speak with your manager or our executive director.

▶ BY-THE-BOOK APPROACH

By-the-Book's personnel policies were developed to facilitate consistent and equitable employment and personnel practices for all employees of the agency. This employee handbook is designed to help employees familiarize themselves with important information about the agency, as well as information regarding their own privileges and responsibilities.

It is not possible to anticipate every situation that may arise in the workplace or to provide information that answers every possible question. Also, future circumstances may require changes in the policies, practices, and benefits described in this handbook. Accordingly, the agency reserves the right to modify, rescind, supplement, or revise any provision in this handbook. The agency will make reasonable efforts to provide employees with advance notice of any modifications or revisions to the handbook and will distribute updated pages as revisions are made.

It is important to note that this handbook only highlights the agency's policies, practices, and benefits and is not intended to be a legal document or contract. The policies and procedures in this

> **CONSIDER THIS**
>
> Take the opportunity to spell out clearly how you expect an employee to use the handbook. This is also the place to state that the policies in the handbook are subject to change, with or without notice. You may choose to state that the policies in the handbook do not constitute or imply any type of employment contract—this slightly strengthens your "at will" employer position.

handbook are intended to replace all previous personnel policies, practices, and guidelines with the exception of the agency's at-will employment policy.

Any questions regarding the contents of this handbook may be addressed to your supervisor or to the director of administration.

▶ LEADING-EDGE APPROACH

This handbook outlines the policies and practices that guide us in our daily work together. We'd like you to know what you can expect from us and what we expect from you.

This handbook was created to serve three primary purposes: to present our policies and practices in one reference source, to conform to certain state and federal laws and convey necessary legal information to our employees, and to give a general description of Leading-Edge's benefits. Nothing contained in this handbook should be perceived as stating or implying a contract of employment.

Underlying what we are communicating in this handbook is Leading-Edge's desire to support individual performance and development and to provide the information necessary for all of us to make good decisions as we go about our daily work.

Please read this entire handbook and sign the acknowledgment at the back within your first two days of employment. You are responsible for knowing its contents and using it as a guide. Of course, you may ask questions about our policies and procedures. Feel free to speak with your supervisor or any member of the human resources staff at any time.

Please keep this handbook. We will notify you from time to time about changes in our policies and practices. The policies, procedures, benefits, and practices described in this handbook should not be taken for granted and are subject to change. We will attempt to give you ample notice when a policy or benefit change is made.

PART TWO

Presenting Clear Employment and Employee Development Policies

CHAPTER TWO

Employment and Hiring Policies

WORK ELIGIBILITY

▶ CREATIVE APPROACH

Typically, on the first day at work, all new staff members will be asked to fill out appropriate forms for payroll purposes and for personnel records. In accordance with the Immigration Reform and Control Act of 1986 (IRCA), all new staff members at Creative Agency are also required as a condition of employment to provide documentation that establishes their identity and their legal right to work in the United States.

▶ BY-THE-BOOK APPROACH

By-the-Book Agency seeks to comply with the requirements of federal law and employs only United States citizens and noncitizens who are lawfully authorized to work in the United States. All employment is conditioned on receipt, by the hiring supervisor or director of administration, of documentation establishing identity and authorization to work in the United States.

▶ LEADING-EDGE APPROACH

Our policy is to employ persons legally entitled to work in the United States without regard to citizenship, ethnic background, or place of national origin. To conform with the Immigration Reform and Control Act of 1986 (IRCA), we hire only those who are eligible to work in the United States. We have adopted the following policies and procedures to encourage compliance with federal regulations and to facilitate our commitment to equal employment opportunity:

1. Except as required by law, no job applicant may be asked about, or categorized according to, citizenship or resident status. Hiring decisions will be made without considering such questions.

CONSIDER THIS

All employers, regardless of size, are required to verify an employee's eligibility to be legally employed in the United States. This must be done within three working days of the employee's start date. Make certain that your new-hire practices include a procedure for viewing and photocopying all appropriate employee documentation and completing INS Form I-90. (Although law does not require photocopies of documents, they are a practical way of providing proof of your compliance with the Immigration Reform and Control Act.)

Be certain, however, not to keep copies of documents or I-90 forms in personnel files—these could be interpreted later as being used as the basis for discrimination. Remember, it is illegal to discriminate in employment on the basis of citizenship or national origin.

2. Applicants offered jobs will be told that they are required to produce satisfactory legal evidence of eligibility to work in the United States—such proof will be a condition of employment.

3. All new employees will be asked to provide actual documents verifying eligibility to work legally in the United States and to complete an INS Form I-9 within three (3) working days.

INTRODUCTORY PERIOD

▶ CREATIVE APPROACH

Your first ninety (90) calendar days of employment are an introductory period. Certain benefits will not be available to you until the completion of this period.

During your introductory period, your manager will observe and talk with you about your job performance. This period also provides you with the opportunity to judge how well your new position suits you.

Your employment is a mutual relationship between you and Creative Agency, which either party may end during or after your introductory period. Completion of your introductory period is not a guarantee of continued employment.

▶ BY-THE-BOOK APPROACH

Employees are considered introductory during the first one hundred eighty (180) days following the date of hire. During this period, performance will be carefully evaluated and a determination made regarding the employee's ability to perform. The fact that an employee has completed the introductory period does not guarantee continued employment. During the introductory period, employees are not eligible to take vacation or paid sick time.

Your employment is a mutual relationship between you and By-the-Book Agency, which either party may end during or after your introductory period.

▶ LEADING-EDGE APPROACH

The introductory period for all employees is meant to provide you and Leading-Edge Agency with an opportunity to evaluate the working relationship. All employees will complete a minimum ninety (90)-day introductory period, and your manager may extend this period beyond ninety (90) days upon review. The introductory period begins with your orientation, which includes a

CONSIDER THIS

Although it is very useful to establish an introductory period as a way of initiating a performance evaluation and for determining when an employee may begin to accrue or use benefits, don't mistake this as an "anything goes" period. You are obligated to follow all state and federal employment laws from the first minute of an employee's first day on the job.

You may want to state here or in your disciplinary policy that any infraction of policy or serious performance problem can be grounds for dismissal during the introductory period—a kind of "one strike and you're out" policy. Further, it's important to convey that no employee is entitled to complete the full introductory period if job performance doesn't support continued employment.

handbook review, and a review of your job description and short-term performance objectives. The remainder of your introductory period is spent increasing your familiarity with the agency and adjusting your skills to your specific job. After thirty (30) days and again at the end of ninety (90) days, you will participate in an evaluation process with your manager. However, feel free to discuss your job description and the contents of this handbook with your manager at any time.

Completion of your introductory period is not a guarantee of continued employment. Your employment is a mutual relationship between you and Leading-Edge Agency, which either party may end during or after your introductory period without cause or advance notice.

EMPLOYEE CLASSIFICATIONS

▶ CREATIVE APPROACH

We place staff members into classifications based on job description, consistent with the Fair Labor Standards Act and applicable state law.

Exempt Employee: An executive, administrative, or professional employee who is exempt from the provisions of the FLSA, usually paid an annual salary

Nonexempt Employee: An employee (generally paid by the hour) who is eligible for overtime pay according to the provisions of the FLSA

Regular Full Time Employee: A salaried or hourly employee who is normally scheduled to work forty (40) hours per workweek and whose employment has no specified end date

Regular Part Time Employee: A salaried or hourly employee who is normally scheduled to work between fifteen (15) and thirty-nine (39) hours per workweek and whose employment has no specified end date

Temporary Employee: An employee who is hired on a full- or part-time basis for a specified period of time, usually not to exceed six (6) months

▶ BY-THE-BOOK APPROACH

We place staff members into classifications based on job description, consistent with the Fair Labor Standards Act and applicable state law.

Exempt Employee: An executive, administrative, or professional employee who is exempt from the provisions of the FLSA, usually paid an annual salary

Nonexempt Employee: An employee (generally paid by the hour) who is eligible for overtime pay according to the provisions of the FLSA

CONSIDER THIS

Many nonprofit managers find it difficult to distinguish between an exempt and a nonexempt employee. In determining which of your positions are which, you must follow the guidelines and exemption tests established by the Fair Labor Standards Act (FLSA) and your state law. The FLSA guidelines are available through the local office of the Employment Development Department. (The Management Center also offers nonprofits a one-page help sheet on exempt versus nonexempt status.) In particular, many employers are not aware of the guidelines governing exempt employee pay. Do not allow exempt employees to take paid time off in half-day or hourly increments. If an exempt employee shows up to work for just one hour, the individual must be paid for a full day of work.

Whereas the law determines which of your employees are exempt and which nonexempt, you determine what constitutes part-time versus full-time work in your organization. Whatever definition suits your organization, it must be applied consistently. Generally, only full-time employees are eligible for health benefits, and part-time employees receive pro-rated paid time off. Each of the three sample policies defines part-time and full-time employees differently.

Regular Full-Time Employee: A salaried or hourly employee who is normally scheduled to work thirty-five (35) hours or more per workweek and whose employment has no specified end date

Regular Part-Time Employee: A salaried or hourly employee who is normally scheduled to work between fifteen (15) and thirty-four (34) hours per workweek and whose employment has no specified end date

Temporary Employee: An employee who is hired on a full- or part-time basis for a specified period of time, usually not to exceed six (6) months

On-Call Employee: A nonexempt employee who is not required to work a specified number of hours in any given workweek but who is scheduled to work on an as-needed basis

Inactive Employee: An employee who is on a leave of absence and is not receiving pay from By-the-Book Agency

▶ LEADING-EDGE APPROACH

Your Leading-Edge Agency employee classification is based on your job description and on the nature of the position, consistent with the Fair Labor Standards Act and all applicable state laws. Your classification determines how you are paid, to what benefits you are entitled, and whether or not you receive overtime pay.

All employees are classified as either exempt or nonexempt, based on their position and the type of work they perform.

Exempt employees hold executive, administrative, professional, or other exempt positions. Exempt employees are generally paid on a salaried basis, and their salary is intended to constitute their entire compensation, regardless of the number of hours they work.

Nonexempt employees perform work that does not meet the qualifications for exemption as defined by the FLSA. Nonexempt employees are generally paid by the hour and are entitled to paid breaks and overtime pay for working over forty (40) hours in one week.

Introductory employees are still working within their introductory period and are not eligible for most benefits until this period is satisfactorily completed.

Full-time employees are those who are assigned a regular work schedule for 37.5 hours or more per workweek and whose assignment is indefinite (does not have a specified end date). Full-time employees are eligible for all employee benefits.

Part-time employees are those who are assigned a regular work schedule of less than 37.5 hours per workweek and whose assignment is indefinite (does not have a specified end date). Part-time employees are eligible for limited employee benefits, excluding medical, dental, and vision coverage.

Temporary full-time or part-time employees are those who are assigned to work for a specified and limited period of time, usually less than six (6) months. Temporary employees are eligible for legally mandated benefits such as workers' compensation insurance and state disability insurance.

Leading-Edge Agency employs consultants and independent contractors from time to time. These individuals are not considered employees and are therefore ineligible for employee benefits, regardless of the length of the employment relationship.

CHANGES IN EMPLOYEE CLASSIFICATIONS

▶ CREATIVE APPROACH

(not necessary in small organizations)

▶ BY-THE-BOOK APPROACH

All employees are classified as regular, temporary, part-time, or full-time, and these classifications determine eligibility for benefits and overtime pay. An employee's classification will not be changed due to a temporary change in work schedule.

Changes in employee classification will occur when a job change, a promotion, or a change in work hours—projected to be ongoing or last for more than four (4) months—takes place.

▶ LEADING-EDGE APPROACH

Your employee classification (which determines eligibility for benefits and overtime pay) may change over the course of your employment with Leading-Edge Agency. If at any time you have a question about a possible change in your classification, please speak with your manager or our director of human resources.

Changes in your employee classification may result from a job change, a promotion, or a change in work hours or your job description. Normally, a temporary change in job duties or work hours—for a period of up to four (4) months—will not affect your employee classification.

POSITION DESCRIPTIONS

► CREATIVE APPROACH

You will receive a position description outlining the primary functions and responsibilities of your job. Your position description is not designed to spell out all the duties and tasks associated with your employment; all our staff members are expected to fulfill both essential and secondary job duties and requirements. Position descriptions are not set in stone and will change, in whole or in part, over time. You are expected to discuss any significant changes in your functions and responsibilities with your manager, who has the authority to formalize changes in position descriptions at his or her discretion.

► BY-THE-BOOK APPROACH

By-the-Book Agency strives to maintain a written job description for all positions. In the event that new paid positions are created through expansion or reorganization, written job descriptions will be prepared and then approved by the executive director before the position is filled.

A job description generally contains the following elements: title, summary of job duties, performance requirements, definition of essential and nonessential functions, qualifications (education, experience, other), title of the immediate supervisor, employee's signature, executive director's signature, and date. Employees may occasionally be required to perform related duties not set forth in the job description. Job descriptions must be rewritten in the event of major new job responsibilities or other significant changes.

► LEADING-EDGE APPROACH

You will have received a position description as part of your orientation process. Read it carefully, and direct any questions you may have to your manager.

Position descriptions are designed to serve three purposes at Leading-Edge Agency. First, they give prospective employees a

CONSIDER THIS

Second only to the time-consuming task of writing a personnel handbook is the creation of job descriptions. I encourage all nonprofits to take the time to develop and keep current job descriptions for each distinct position in the organization, because job descriptions are the basis for many critical employment processes, including hiring, promotion, and performance evaluation.

Job descriptions have many uses. To comply with the Americans with Disabilities Act, it is necessary to identify the essential functions of each job. Job descriptions are the basis of the hiring process and should be the foundation of a performance evaluation.

Don't think of a job description as a list of tasks or activities. Job descriptions should highlight the essential functions and the primary outcomes of the job. They should answer the question "Why does this job exist?" rather than "What does this person do all day?" Be sure not to build the job description around an individual—it describes the job, not the person who does it.

A sample job description can be found in the Resources section at the back of this book.

clear understanding of the nature of an open position and facilitate the recruitment process. Second, they serve as guidelines for employees already working in established positions. Third, they assist Leading-Edge in complying with the Americans with Disabilities Act by identifying the essential functions and physical requirements of each of our positions.

Position descriptions are dynamic documents, meant to be updated and revised continuously, based on the programs and services we offer. Generally, position descriptions are reviewed and revised as part of our annual performance appraisal process. We encourage you to offer suggestions for improving your effectiveness and the design of your position by speaking with your manager or our director of human resources.

JOB POSTINGS

▶ CREATIVE APPROACH

(not common practice to spell out this policy in a small organization)

▶ BY-THE-BOOK APPROACH

It is the policy of By-the-Book Agency to find the most qualified candidates to fill position vacancies. This will be accomplished through a combination of internal and external recruiting. Consideration will be given to the advancement of current employees, and employees are encouraged to apply for promotions or transfers for which they feel they are qualified.

Open positions may be posted for seven (7) calendar days on bulletin boards at the discretion of the director of administration or the executive director. The decision to fill positions from within or to hire from outside is made solely by By-the-Book Agency.

Only the director of administration and the executive director have the authority to extend job offers. All offers of employment will be in writing.

▶ LEADING-EDGE APPROACH

Our employment policy at Leading-Edge Agency is to select the most qualified person available for a position based on knowledge, skills, experience, and ability to perform job requirements. We are dedicated to internal promotion. We post all open positions internally, usually before any external posting or advertising begins. No hiring decision is made before all qualified internal applicants have been interviewed. In the case of a choice between equally qualified candidates, internal applicants will be given preferential consideration.

Currently open positions are posted on specially designated bulletin boards. Descriptions of any position in the organization are available from our human resources department. If you are interested in an open position, you may request a confidential

CONSIDER THIS

Many employees are concerned about losing an opportunity for advancement to an outside hire. Carefully think through your own philosophy on internal transfers and promotions, and craft a policy that you can live with. Few policies are scrutinized more by employees than those concerning job postings.

exploratory meeting with a member of our human resources staff before deciding to apply. Once you are an official candidate, you are required to tell your current manager of your interest in the other position, as your supervisor may be asked to give the hiring manager a reference regarding your current job performance.

EMPLOYEE REFERRAL BONUS PROGRAMS

▶ CREATIVE APPROACH

(not common in small organizations because of the risk of creating too in-bred a staff)

▶ BY-THE-BOOK APPROACH

(see Leading-Edge Approach)

▶ LEADING-EDGE APPROACH

Leading-Edge's Referral Bonus Program encourages staff members to refer qualified external applicants for employment. Any current Leading-Edge employee who refers a successful candidate for an open position will receive a paid day off, to be used within three (3) months of the referral's first day on the job.

Speak with our human resources director for more information about the program. Members of the human resources staff, the executive director, and the direct hiring manager for a given opening are not eligible to participate in the Referral Bonus Program.

CONSIDER THIS

Referral bonus programs for employees are a terrific idea. In today's labor market, it is increasingly difficult to attract qualified applicants, especially for entry-level positions. A referral bonus program provides an incentive for your employees to act as contingency recruiters—and who knows your organization better than they do?

HIRING OF RELATIVES

CONSIDER THIS

Having this policy is like carrying an umbrella so that it won't rain: it's agencies without such a policy that end up wishing they had created one.

▶ CREATIVE APPROACH

We have no prohibition against hiring relatives of our staff members. However, one general restriction has been established to help ensure fair treatment of all staff members. Although we will accept and consider applications for employment from relatives, they will not be hired for, promoted to, or transferred into positions in which there is a direct or indirect supervisory relationship between family members.

▶ BY-THE-BOOK APPROACH

To foster an environment in which integrity and objectivity can be maintained, the By-the-Book Agency does not permit the employment of members of the same family in the same department.

For purposes of this policy, the term *family* applies to the following relationships, based on blood, marriage, or other definitions: parent-child, sibling, grandparent-grandchild, aunt/uncle–niece/nephew, stepmother/father–stepchild, cousin, or spouse-spouse or spousal equivalent.

By-the-Book does not permit an employee to work under the immediate supervision of a member of the same family. If such situations now exist or if they develop in the future because of promotion, marriage, transfer, or any other reason, the management of By-the-Book reserves the right to transfer or terminate either or both employees, if necessary.

▶ LEADING-EDGE APPROACH

It is our policy to avoid bringing family relationships into the workplace whenever possible. However, on occasion, more than one family member may work for Leading-Edge Agency. The following guidelines will govern these situations:

1. No employee will be permitted to hire a relative.
2. When related persons work for Leading-Edge, one relative may not supervise another.

3. Related persons will not be involved in evaluating each other's job performance or in making recommendations for salary adjustments, promotions, or other budget decisions.

For the purposes of this policy, the term *family member* includes individuals related more closely than second cousins by blood or marriage or unrelated persons sharing the same household.

EMPLOYMENT OF BOARD MEMBERS

▶ ALL APPROACHES

To preserve the objectivity and integrity of the agency's board of directors, any member who wishes to apply for employment with the agency must first resign from the board.

CHAPTER THREE

Employee Development

PERFORMANCE EVALUATIONS

► CREATIVE APPROACH

In addition to your ninety (90)-day performance review at the completion of your introductory period, you will participate with your manager in an annual performance review process. As part of this annual process, you and your manager will assess your accomplishments during the previous year and set new performance goals for the coming year.

► BY-THE-BOOK APPROACH

Each employee's performance will be reviewed on a continual basis by his or her immediate supervisor. A formal year-end performance appraisal will be conducted, to coincide with the end of the agency's fiscal year. Although the mechanics of the performance appraisal process may change from time to time, it will always include the components of planning, goal setting, measurement, communication, and feedback.

Annual performance appraisals, signed by both employee and supervisor, are placed in the employee's personnel file. Employees may keep a copy of their appraisal and have the opportunity to comment on it in writing. Performance appraisal also includes a discussion about career planning and development.

► LEADING-EDGE APPROACH

The annual performance evaluation process at Leading-Edge Agency is an opportunity for a regular and periodic review of your job performance. During the evaluation process, you and your manager will assess your performance in relation to objectives you have previously agreed on and identify areas of strength and areas needing development. In addition, you and your supervisor will develop goals and objectives for the next review period and identify the ways in which your supervisor will support your further development.

CONSIDER THIS

Although not required by law, performance evaluations are an important tool for clarifying performance standards, encouraging skill development, and emphasizing key organizational values. Performance evaluations are an essential component of any pay-for-performance system.

The agency's annual performance evaluation process, which takes place at the close of our fiscal year, is based on the following principles:

- Performance goal setting and evaluation are two-way processes involving both employee and supervisor.
- Employee performance is evaluated on objective, job-related criteria that have been communicated to you in advance.

Setting goals and objectives for future performance is as important as evaluating past performance. The objectives of Leading-Edge's performance evaluation process are as follows:

1. To let our employees know how they are doing on the job
2. To encourage communication and two-way feedback on the expectations and goals of both employees and the agency
3. To provide a fair and consistent method for making pay decisions
4. To document performance in ways that will assist future supervisors and facilitate transfers, promotions, and improvement plans
5. To serve as a tool for coaching, planning, and professional development

At Leading-Edge, we believe that it is important for our employees to know exactly how well they are doing in relation to our established standards of performance.

TRANSFERS AND PROMOTIONS

▶ ALL APPROACHES

To be eligible to apply for a transfer or promotion, an employee must have been in his or her current position for at least six (6) months and must be meeting the requirements of the current position. Employees on a written warning dealing with job performance or unacceptable behavior are ineligible for transfers or promotions. The executive director must approve any exceptions to these policies.

CONSIDER THIS

If you are a small agency, you may not need to have a formal policy about transfers and promotions. In larger organizations, it's a good idea to determine how long an employee must be in one job before applying for another. Larger organizations also find it helpful to specify that employees on written warning are not eligible for transfers (to avoid transferring a problem from one department to another).

EDUCATION AND PROFESSIONAL DEVELOPMENT

CONSIDER THIS

If you pay for outside training and education, it is very important to create clear guidelines about who is eligible and how to initiate the approval process. You want to encourage employees to develop themselves professionally, but you do not want to create inequities in the way such a policy is put into practice by inadvertently favoring one class or education level over another.

▶ CREATIVE APPROACH

(not common practice in small organizations)

▶ BY-THE-BOOK APPROACH

By-the-Book Agency supports employees who wish to enhance their professional development and job-related skills through external education programs and conferences. In addition, employees may be asked to attend conferences and training forums as participants or presenters. Employees must have the prior approval of their supervisor to attend outside development events.

By-the-Book covers the costs of outside training and conferences based on organizational benefit and annual budget. All agency-covered training and conferences require the approval of the executive director and are subject to change based on budgetary constraints.

▶ LEADING-EDGE APPROACH

In addition to on-the-job learning and training, Leading-Edge encourages employees to enhance professional development and job-related skills through external education programs and conferences. Up to five (5) paid days per calendar year are provided for regular full-time employees who wish to enhance job-related skills by, for example, attending external training programs and seminars. Educational leave does not carry over from year to year. Time off (whether paid or unpaid) for external training and continuing education requires advance approval by the employee's supervisor.

Employees may be asked to attend conferences, workshops, and educational meetings on behalf of the agency. In these instances, Leading-Edge will cover most travel, lodging, registration, and meal expenses. Employees will receive regular pay while attending required outside conferences. Days spent attending required educational or professional development events will not be deducted from annual educational leave.

Although we do not cover the cost of continuing education for our employees, we will attempt to accommodate continuing education through flexible scheduling for employees who are attending school while working.

PART THREE

Creating Well-Crafted Benefits Policies

CHAPTER FOUR

Health, Wellness, and Employee Assistance

HEALTH INSURANCE

▶ CREATIVE APPROACH

At Creative Agency, we believe that our staff members should have access to health insurance coverage for themselves and their dependents. We strive to provide all our staff members with adequate health care benefits and work in partnership with our health care providers to ensure access for all our staff members.

Full-time staff members and their dependents are eligible for medical and dental coverage through our HMO. Creative Agency pays 100 percent of the premiums for all full-time staff, and we pay 25 percent of the premiums for eligible dependents.

Part-time staff members are eligible to apply for medical coverage through an alternative health care provider; the cost of premiums for our part-time staff members and their dependents is borne entirely by them.

As with most policies, our benefits coverage is subject to change. For more information about health care coverage, please speak with our office manager.

▶ BY-THE-BOOK APPROACH

MEDICAL INSURANCE

Eligible full-time employees may choose from two medical coverage options. The cost of medical insurance is shared by the employee and By-the-Book Agency. Coverage begins on the first day of the month following completion of the introductory period. Coverage ends on the last day of the month in which the employee is employed.

DENTAL INSURANCE

Dental insurance is available on a shared-cost basis. Coverage begins on the first day of the month following completion of the introductory period. Coverage ends on the last day of the month in which the employee is employed.

CONSIDER THIS

There are almost as many health plan options as there are nonprofits, and a discussion about choosing among them is beyond the scope of this handbook.

You should choose employee health insurance benefits and cost-sharing options specifically tailored to the needs and resources of your organization. The three examples provided here are designed to give you an idea of how health insurance benefits can vary from one organization to another.

As with most policies, benefits coverage is subject to change. Please speak to the office manager if you have questions about medical or dental insurance.

▶ LEADING-EDGE APPROACH

HEALTH AND WELLNESS

Leading-Edge Agency establishes a health and wellness account for each of our full-time employees. After completing thirty (30) days of employment, each full-time employee receives a monthly health and wellness deposit equal to health coverage costs for the employee through one of the three health care plans the agency offers.

Upon completion of six (6) months of satisfactory continuous employment, our full-time employees with eligible dependents receive an additional monthly deposit equal to 50 percent of the cost of dependent coverage (through the same health care plan).

COVERAGE OPTION

If an employee has medical coverage from another source, such as a spouse's medical plan, the employee may apply the monthly amount Leading-Edge would normally spend on the medical insurance premium to a wellness account. Proof of health insurance coverage from an outside source is required for participation in the wellness account.

An employee participating in the coverage option may use the monthly income in one of two ways:

1. Place it in the agency's 401(3b) savings plan
2. Apply it to the cost of a monthly health club membership

DEFINITIONS FOR ELIGIBILITY

▶ CREATIVE APPROACH

For the purposes of benefits coverage, Creative Agency defines "immediate family" as a spouse or domestic partner, children (including stepchildren and foster children), parents, and siblings.

For the purposes of benefits coverage, we define "domestic partnership" as an eligible staff member and one other person sharing a committed relationship that includes living together, financial interdependence, joint responsibility for each other's common welfare, and each considering the other to be a life partner.

Note: These definitions pertain only to specific benefits; eligibility for these benefits is described on the following pages.

▶ BY-THE-BOOK APPROACH

For the purposes of benefits coverage, "immediate family" is defined as spouse or partner, parents, parents-in-law, siblings, children, grandchildren, and grandparents.

▶ LEADING-EDGE APPROACH

Certain benefits, such as health insurance coverage, family care leave, and bereavement leave, use the term "immediate family" or "domestic partner" in descriptions of eligibility or coverage. At Leading-Edge, we define "immediate family" as your spouse or domestic partner, children (including stepchildren and foster children), siblings (including stepsiblings and siblings-in-law), parents (including stepparents and parents-in-law), grandparents, and grandchildren.

At Leading-Edge, we recognize domestic partners as spousal equivalents, providing that both the employee and domestic partner satisfy the following requirements:

- They are eighteen (18) years of age or older.
- They are unmarried.
- They are not related to each other.

CONSIDER THIS

Everyone's definition of "immediate family" might differ, so it's best to set out a formal definition for the purposes of benefits eligibility—in the case of bereavement leave, for example, or for sick time to be used to care for a member of the family.

Even if you do not offer health insurance coverage to domestic partners, it is helpful to define the term for other benefits, such as bereavement leave, family care leave, or use of sick time.

- They share an intimate, committed relationship of mutual caring of at least six (6) months' duration.
- They live together.
- They agree to be responsible for each other's basic living expenses.
- They do not currently have a different domestic partner.
- They have executed a Declaration of Domestic Partnership affidavit.

INSURANCE CONTINUATION

▶ CREATIVE APPROACH

The Consolidated Omnibus Budget Reconciliation Act of 1986 (COBRA) guarantees continuous coverage of health and dental insurance to eligible employees and their dependents (at the employee's expense) at group rates that otherwise might have been forfeited when employment ends.

At the time of the creation of this manual, Creative Agency did not qualify for COBRA coverage because of our size. If this status changes, we will notify all staff members.

Our health insurance carrier does offer a conversion coverage plan to all staff members at the time of termination of employment. If you are covered by our health insurance and leave our employ, the carrier will notify you of the option and cost of continuous coverage.

▶ BY-THE-BOOK APPROACH

Upon termination, employees covered under a health insurance plan have certain legal rights to remain on the insurance plan at their own expense for up to eighteen (18) months (more in some exceptional cases) through COBRA benefits. More information regarding COBRA coverage, costs, and administrative procedures is available from the finance department at the time employment ends or when an employee has a question about other qualifying events.

▶ LEADING-EDGE APPROACH

(policy is legally mandated; see By-the-Book Approach)

CONSIDER THIS

A handbook is not the place to spell out all the details and guidelines for insurance continuation. Insurance continuation is mandated by the Consolidated Omnibus Budget Reconciliation Act of 1986 (COBRA). The handbook should inform employees of their basic right to continuation; more detailed information should be provided at the time of eligibility.

Employers with twenty or more employees are required to offer insurance continuation under COBRA. You may check with your insurance carrier about your options for voluntarily offering insurance continuation.

Because COBRA regulations require employers to follow complex procedures and to adhere to strict timelines, COBRA administration should be assigned to a qualified administrator or manager in your organization.

WORKERS' COMPENSATION

CONSIDER THIS

Workers' compensation is legally mandated in all states. In addition to the basic information in your handbook, you should train all employees in the basics of preventing and responding to on-the-job injuries. Most workers' compensation insurance carriers provide safety training videos and educational information to client organizations. Ask about your carrier's training and education programs. (See also Chapter Eight, "Workplace Health and Safety.")

▶ CREATIVE APPROACH

Our staff members are protected by workers' compensation insurance for all illness or injury arising from and occurring within the scope of their employment.

If you are injured on the job, notify your manager immediately, no matter how minor the injury may seem.

It is our policy to return an injured staff member to work as soon as possible on modified or light-duty status until the time that a physician's release to return to regular work is obtained.

▶ BY-THE-BOOK APPROACH

By-the-Book Agency carries workers' compensation insurance as required by law to protect employees who are injured on the job. This insurance provides medical, surgical, and hospital treatment in addition to compensation for loss of pay resulting from work-related injuries or illness. The cost of this coverage is paid by the agency.

You must immediately report any on-the-job injury to your supervisor, regardless of how minor the injury may seem. Questions concerning our workers' compensation coverage should be directed to the office manager.

By-the-Book does not provide workers' compensation coverage for injuries sustained during or as a result of an employee's voluntary participation in off-duty social, recreational, or athletic activities that are not part of an employee's work-related duties. If an employee is required or expected to participate in a recreational, social, or athletic activity as part of his or her job, however, workers' compensation coverage may apply.

▶ LEADING-EDGE APPROACH

All employees are protected by our workers' compensation insurance policy while employed at Leading-Edge Agency. The policy is available at no cost to you and covers injury or illness resulting from legitimate work activities. By law, we are required to report injuries covered under workers' compensation within twenty-four (24) hours. Please report any on-the-job injury to your manager or a member of the human resources staff immediately.

Complete information about workers' compensation and on-the-job injuries is available from our human resources department.

DISABILITY INSURANCE

Employees are often confused about the differences in benefits offered by workers' compensation insurance, group medical insurance, and available state disability insurance plans. Designate someone in your organization as the benefits expert, and make sure that all your employees know they can speak with that person to get answers to their health insurance questions.

▶ CREATIVE APPROACH

Each of our staff members contributes to state disability insurance. Contributions are made through payroll deductions. State disability insurance is payable when you cannot work because of illness or injury not related to employment, when you are unable to work for reasons related to pregnancy, or when you are entitled to workers' compensation at a rate that is less than your daily disability benefit amount.

Coverage begins on your first day of employment and ends on your last. For more information about state disability insurance, please speak with our office manager.

▶ BY-THE-BOOK APPROACH

Employees of By-the-Book Agency who are unable to work due to illness, injury, or pregnancy may receive state-funded income protection insurance for the time they are unable to work. The determination of benefits is up to the state. An employee may apply for disability benefits after being disabled for eight (8) days, or if hospitalized, after one (1) day of disability. Forms can be obtained from the director of operations, the local office of the Employment Development Department, or the employee's physician.

If a physician deems an employee to be temporarily disabled, the employee cannot return to work without first submitting a medical release to his or her supervisor.

▶ LEADING-EDGE APPROACH

SHORT-TERM DISABILITY (STD)

Each of our staff members contributes to state disability insurance. Contributions are made through payroll deductions. State disability insurance is payable when you cannot work because of illness or injury not related to employment, when you are unable to work for reasons related to pregnancy, or when you are entitled to workers' compensation at a rate that is less than your daily disability benefit amount.

Coverage begins on your first day of employment and ends on your last. For more information about state disability insurance, please speak with our office manager.

LONG-TERM DISABILITY (LTD)

Leading-Edge Agency provides LTD coverage at the agency's expense to ensure that you receive a percentage of your salary if you must miss work due to a disability. You are eligible for LTD coverage following your ninety (90)-day introductory period. LTD benefits begin after ninety (90) days of continuous doctor-certified disability. Your benefit is equal to 60 percent of your predisability base pay. LTD benefits coordinate with other disability programs.

Please contact our human resources department as soon as possible after a disabling event to receive more information about this coverage.

LIFE INSURANCE

▶ CREATIVE APPROACH

All regular full-time staff members are covered under our life insurance plan. The plan offers a benefit equal to your annual base salary or annualized hourly wage. You must delegate a beneficiary to whom this benefit will be paid in the event of your death. Creative Agency pays for the full premium for this benefit.

▶ BY-THE-BOOK APPROACH

Regular full-time employees are eligible for a basic life and accidental death and dismemberment insurance plan paid for by the agency. Employees may elect supplemental coverage as well as dependent life insurance coverage at their own expense. Coverage begins on the first day of the month after one (1) full month of employment and ends on the last day of the month in which employment ends.

▶ LEADING-EDGE APPROACH

(see policies outlined for the other approaches)

FLEXIBLE SPENDING ACCOUNT

▶ ALL APPROACHES

All regular full- and part-time staff members may choose to enroll in our flexible spending account program, which allows staff members to set aside pretax dollars to be used for uninsured medical expenses (such as your out-of-pocket amount or vision care) or dependent care services.

Essentially, this benefit allows you to stretch your income a bit by using tax-free dollars to pay for medical expenses not covered by insurance and for child care and other eligible dependent care expenses.

PROCEDURE

- Eligible staff members may enroll in the program upon hire or at the start of a new plan year. The plan year normally runs from June 1 to May 31. Enrollment forms are available from our office manager.

- Money is automatically taken out of each paycheck; no taxes are withheld from this amount.

- Staff members submit receipts for reimbursement to our office manager; reimbursements are made on a monthly basis for health care expenses and on a biweekly basis for dependent care.

A WORD OF CAUTION

No refunds of money left in an individual's spending account are given at the end of the plan year. This means that staff members participating in the plan need to estimate expenses carefully. Money remaining in all staff members' FSAs at the end of the plan year is pooled and divided equally among the accounts of continuing participants who also participated in the plan during the previous year.

Please see our office manager for more information regarding flexible spending accounts.

CONSIDER THIS

This is a good benefit to offer employees, especially if you have numerous employees with young children or if you require a shared health care premium or your health insurance out-of-pocket deductible is high.

Flexible spending accounts (FSAs) allow employees to set aside pretax dollars to pay for planned expenses such as child care and uninsured health care costs.

You can offer this benefit at little cost to your organization. If you are interested in offering an FSA, consult with your accountant.

EMPLOYEE ASSISTANCE PROGRAM

▶ CREATIVE APPROACH

(not common due to cost, although special arrangements can be made in individual cases)

▶ BY-THE-BOOK APPROACH

(not common due to cost, although special arrangements can be made in individual cases)

▶ LEADING-EDGE APPROACH

There may be occasions when an employee's work performance is jeopardized by unresolved personal problems. Examples of this include financial crisis, family difficulties, drug or alcohol abuse, and gambling. Leading-Edge Agency's policy is to make it possible for the individual employee to get the help needed to restore job effectiveness.

We will make available, on a confidential basis through our human resources department, the phone number of a professional, confidential counseling service, the services of which are paid for by the agency. No employee's job security or promotional opportunity will be jeopardized because he or she has sought and conscientiously followed a program of treatment.

Voluntary acceptance of a treatment program is not a valid reason for continued poor job performance. Poor job performance resulting from apparent behavior or personal problems is handled in the same manner as any other substandard performance.

Reporting to work under the influence of drugs or alcohol, or possessing drugs or alcohol on our property, will result in immediate termination.

Employees who suspect they have a problem are urged to take advantage of our employee assistance program and to follow through with any recommended treatment.

ELDER CARE

▶ CREATIVE APPROACH

(not common due to cost)

▶ BY-THE-BOOK APPROACH

(not common due to cost)

▶ LEADING-EDGE APPROACH

If you have the regular responsibility of providing care for an elderly relative, we encourage you to take advantage of our flexible scheduling arrangements. You may use accrued personal use time to care for an elderly parent or relative.

Through our flexible spending account program you may be able to set aside tax-free dollars to use for expenses associated with the care of an elderly dependent. Please see our human resources department for more information.

If you anticipate needing significant or regular amounts of time off because of a parent's serious health condition, please consult the "Leaves of Absence" section of this handbook, which details our family and medical leave policy.

CONSIDER THIS

An increasing number of employees are responsible for providing some care for an elderly parent. This type of benefit is greatly appreciated by employees who sometimes get left out of the picture when it comes to dependent care benefits.

NEW BABY

▶ CREATIVE APPROACH

(not common due to cost)

▶ BY-THE-BOOK APPROACH

(not common due to cost)

▶ LEADING-EDGE APPROACH

Employees who are welcoming a newborn or newly adopted child receive a $100 Treasury certificate for future financial assistance. The certificate is redeemable when the child reaches eighteen (18) years of age. Employees are responsible for filling out the "New Addition to My Family" form available from the human resources department.

CREDIT UNION

▶ CREATIVE AGENCY

(not common practice in small organizations)

▶ BY-THE-BOOK APPROACH

By-the-Book has established an affiliation with a local credit union. The credit union offers employees a range of savings, investment, and loan options at favorable interest rates. Payroll deduction is available for employees who wish to make regular monthly contributions. Information and forms are available from the finance director.

▶ LEADING-EDGE APPROACH

We participate in the State Name Credit Union. Membership is available to all Leading-Edge Agency employees. Most transactions, including joining the credit union, can be conducted through the mail or by phone. Information on the financial services available through State Name Credit Union and on applying for membership is available from the human resources department.

CONSIDER THIS

It costs you very little to offer employees credit union membership. It's a particularly helpful benefit to younger employees who may be buying a first car or first home.

CHAPTER FIVE

Paid Time Off

VACATIONS

▶ CREATIVE APPROACH

We offer paid vacation time to eligible staff members for their rest and recreation away from work. Creative Agency recognizes the value of time away from work responsibilities and encourages staff members to use all accrued vacation benefits on a timely basis.

Because we believe that time away from work is beneficial for rest and rejuvenation, we do not allow staff members to take pay in lieu of vacation time.

ELIGIBILITY

All regular staff members who work an average of thirty-five (35) hours per week or more begin to accrue vacation time on the first day of employment; however, staff members may not take time off for vacation until they complete six (6) months of continuous service.

ACCRUAL

Regular full-time staff members earn paid vacation at their regular rate of pay, computed hourly, as follows:

Length of Service	Hours per Pay Period	Hours per Year
0–12 months	3.077	80
13–36 months	5	120
37 or more months	6.67	160

Regular part-time staff members—those who work fifteen (15) or more hours per week—earn paid vacation on a prorated basis, determined by the number of hours they are regularly scheduled to work per week.

MAXIMUM ACCRUAL

All eligible staff members are expected to use accrued vacation benefits each year. Regular full-time staff members cannot accrue more vacation than they earn in twelve (12) months. Only after some accrued vacation time is used will new vacation time begin

CONSIDER THIS

Most employers now mandate some type of limit, or "cap," on vacation accruals, to prevent employees from building up huge reserves of paid vacation. Not only are large amounts of paid vacation time difficult to schedule, but it can be hard on an employer's budget to pay out large amounts of accrued vacation when an employee leaves. Caps are also useful in preventing burnout in employees who can never find the time to take a vacation (especially when they know they can keep accruing it indefinitely).

Some states' laws prohibit employers from adopting a "use it or lose it" policy; you cannot take away vacation time once it has been accrued. You can cap accruals at a certain level and require accrued vacation to be used before additional time begins accruing. Although vacation pay is not a legally required benefit, all employers should encourage employees to plan for and take regular vacations as one way of balancing work and personal life.

accruing again. Exceptions to this policy, based on extraordinary circumstances, require the approval of the staff member's manager and the executive director.

SCHEDULING

Accrued vacation may be taken after completion of the first six (6) months of employment. Vacation requests must be made at least thirty (30) days in advance and require the approval of the executive director. Conflicting requests will be decided by length of service.

▶ BY-THE-BOOK APPROACH

Regular full-time employees earn paid vacation time on the following schedule, beginning with the first day of employment:

1–3 years:	12 days each calendar year (90 hours)
4–10 years:	15 days each calendar year (120 hours)
11 + years:	20 days each calendar year (150 hours)

Regular part-time employees scheduled to work twenty (20) or more hours per week earn paid vacation time on a prorated basis based on the number of hours worked per week.

No other classification of employee earns paid vacation time.

At the end of each calendar year, employees may carry over accrued, unused vacation pay. However, employees must take accrued and carried-over vacation by April 1 of the following year in order to continue to accrue additional vacation time.

In extraordinary circumstances when vacation cannot be taken in the approved time frame, the executive director may grant approval to carry over time beyond the allotted period while regular accrual continues.

All vacation time must be requested and approved in advance. Employees with five (5) or more years of service may take vacation time for the current year in advance of its being accrued.

Employees may not receive pay in lieu of vacation. When they leave the organization, employees will be paid for any accrued, unused vacation.

▶ LEADING-EDGE APPROACH

We encourage employees to take vacations to refresh themselves and to ensure the high quality of their work.

FULL-TIME EMPLOYEES

As a full-time employee, you earn up to fifteen (15) paid vacation days each year. Paid vacation time is accrued on a monthly basis at the rate of 1.25 vacation days per month. You begin to earn vacation time on your first day of employment, but you must complete six (6) months of employment before using accrued vacation.

PART-TIME EMPLOYEES

As a part-time employee, you earn paid vacation days on a prorated basis each year, based on the standard of fifteen (15) days for 2,080 hours of work annually. You begin to earn vacation time on your first day of employment, but you must complete six (6) months of employment before using accrued vacation.

ACCRUAL MAXIMUM

Vacation time can accrue to a maximum of twenty (20) days. Once this cap is reached, no further vacation time will accrue until some vacation is used. There is no retroactive grant of vacation time for the period when accrued vacation compensation was at the cap. Any exceptions to this policy require the written approval of our executive director.

ADDITION VACATION

Employees who have completed five (5) years of service accrue an additional day of vacation for each year of employment, to a maximum of thirty (30) days of annual vacation. For example, if you have completed five (5) years of employment, you accrue twenty (20) days of vacation annually: fifteen (15) days plus an additional five (5).

SCHEDULING

You are expected to exercise consideration and good judgment when requesting vacation days from your manager. If you request vacation during a particularly busy time or at a time when many others have also requested time off, you may be required to postpone your vacation. Generally, we ask that you request vacation time at least thirty (30) days in advance.

HOLIDAYS

CONSIDER THIS

If you have a diverse workforce, it is a good idea to build some flexibility into your paid holiday benefit by offering personal days or optional paid holidays.

On a practical note, identifying in advance when you will observe holidays that fall on weekends assists your employees in planning family time and other personal matters.

You are not legally required to offer paid holidays. The following examples show typical holidays offered by non-profits, but you may choose to offer different paid holidays, based on your organization's needs.

▶ CREATIVE APPROACH

All regular staff members receive paid time off for the following holidays:

New Year's Day	Martin Luther King Jr. Day
Presidents Day	Memorial Day
Independence Day	Labor Day
Thanksgiving Day	Friday after Thanksgiving
Christmas Eve	Christmas Day

Regular part-time staff members receive holiday pay on a pro-rated basis.

▶ BY-THE-BOOK APPROACH

The executive director at the beginning of our fiscal year publishes the holiday schedule. By-the-Book Agency observes the following holidays:

New Year's Day	Martin Luther King Jr. Day
Presidents Day	Memorial Day
Independence Day	Labor Day
Thanksgiving Day	Friday after Thanksgiving
Christmas Eve	Christmas Day

All regular full-time employees are paid eight (8) hours' wages for each holiday. Regular part-time employees are paid for holidays on a prorated basis, determined by the number of hours worked in a workweek. Part-time employees who do not work on the day on which a holiday falls may observe the holiday on a different day of the week by arranging for this in advance with their supervisor.

Any nonexempt employees required to work on a holiday will be paid at one and one-half (1.5) times their regular rate of pay for hours worked that day and will be granted paid time off on another day equivalent to the number of hours worked on the holiday. This alternative paid time off must be taken within one (1) month of the holiday worked.

Any exempt employees required to work on a holiday will be paid at one and one-half (1.5) times their regular rate of pay for that day and will be granted an alternative paid day off, to be taken within one (1) month of the holiday worked.

Temporary employees do not receive holiday pay.

Employees on vacation at the time a holiday occurs will not have that day counted as vacation pay.

▶ LEADING-EDGE APPROACH

We offer our employees paid holidays throughout the year to facilitate participation in national holidays and to provide opportunities for celebration of religious and ethnic holidays.

The following are official holidays for all Leading-Edge Agency employees. Our offices will be closed on these days:

New Year's Day	Martin Luther King Jr. Day
Memorial Day	Independence Day
Labor Day	Thanksgiving Day
Friday after Thanksgiving	Christmas Day

Full- and part-time employees who regularly work at least twenty (20) hours per week receive holiday pay for the days listed above. Temporary employees and part-time employees who work less than twenty (20) hours per week take these days off without pay.

Eligible part-time employees who do not work on the day on which a holiday falls may observe the holiday on a different day of the week by arranging for this in advance with their supervisor.

When a holiday falls on a Saturday, the office will be closed on the preceding Friday to observe the holiday. When a holiday falls on a Sunday, the office will be closed on the following Monday to observe the holiday.

All eligible employees also may choose two additional holidays from the following list, for a total of ten (10) paid holidays per year.

Optional Holidays

Employee's birthday	Employee's wedding anniversary
Christmas Eve	Kwanzaa
Valentine's Day	Chinese New Year
Fiesta San Jacinto	St. Patrick's Day
Good Friday	Emancipation Day
Cinco de Mayo	Yom Kippur
Rosh Hashanah	Fiestas Patrias
Dia de los Muertos	

FLOATING PERSONAL DAYS

▶ CREATIVE APPROACH

Personal days are for use at your discretion for personal business or to allow you to observe additional religious or ethnic holidays. Personal days cannot be combined with vacation time.

Regular full-time staff members earn one (1) paid personal day for every six (6) months worked. Personal days are accrued as of your hire date initially and thereafter on January 1 and July 1 of every calendar year.

Regular part-time staff members earn one (1) paid personal day per calendar year of service.

Personal days cannot be carried over from year to year; if you do not use them, you lose them. You are not paid for accrued, unused personal days when your employment at Creative Agency ends.

▶ BY-THE-BOOK APPROACH

In addition to paid holidays, two (2) floating holidays are provided each year to regular full-time employees, to be used for special occasions such as birthdays or ethnic or religious holidays. Regular full-time employees earn two (2) floating holidays in their first year if they are employed before July 1; after July 1, one (1) floating holiday in their first year. In succeeding years, employees are granted two (2) floating holidays per year.

Regular part-time employees who are scheduled to work twenty (20) hours or more per week are eligible for floating days at the rate of one-half of the full-time rate.

Temporary or part-time employees working less than twenty (20) hours per week do not receive floating holidays.

Floating holidays must be used in the calendar year in which they are granted. Employees will be paid for floating days not used when they leave the organization.

▶ LEADING-EDGE APPROACH

(see policy for Personal Use Time)

CONSIDER THIS

Whether you call them personal days, floating holidays, or floating personal days, it's a good idea to offer employees flexible paid days off to accommodate personal responsibilities, religious holidays, and family obligations.

SICK TIME

▶ CREATIVE APPROACH

We provide paid sick time to regular full- and part-time staff members to provide you with protection against loss of income if you are ill or injured or if you need time off from work for necessary or routine health care.

ACCRUAL

Regular full-time staff members earn sick time at the rate of eight (8) hours per month of work.

Regular part-time staff members earn sick time on a prorated basis, determined by the number of hours worked per week.

Staff members may accrue up to a maximum of twenty-four (24) days of sick time. Upon reaching the maximum, no further sick time will be accrued until some of the accrued time has been used.

USE

Staff members who are ill or injured and anticipate being away from work for more than one (1) week should speak with their health care provider or our office manager for information about state disability income benefits.

Under some circumstances, we may require verification of a staff member's medical condition, especially if a pattern of frequently used sick time develops.

PAYMENT

We do not offer pay in lieu of use of accrued sick time, and staff members do not receive payment for accrued sick time when they leave our employ.

▶ BY-THE-BOOK APPROACH

Sick time provides regular full- and part-time employees with paid time off to recover from illness or injury. Sick time may also be used by regular part-time employees for health care appointments that cannot be scheduled outside work hours.

ACCRUAL AND PAYMENT

Regular full-time employees accrue sick time at the rate of one (1) day per month of service for a total of twelve (12) days per year. Regular part-time employees accrue sick time on a prorated basis, based on the number of hours they regularly work per month.

Sick time may be carried over from one year to the next, but accrual caps at 60 days until some sick time is used.

Sick time is accrued from the start of employment but cannot be used until the employee has satisfactorily completed the introductory period.

No payment is made for accrued, unused sick time upon separation.

SICK TIME USE

Employees are responsible for directly notifying their supervisor when prevented from starting or continuing a workday due to illness or injury. Employees must also keep their supervisor informed about the expected duration of the time away from work.

In most circumstances, a doctor's statement is required when an employee uses more than five (5) consecutive days of sick time or when an accumulation of absences seems to establish (in the supervisor's judgment) a problematic use of sick time. By-the-Book may request verification of the reasons for any use of sick time.

Employees may use sick time to care for ill family members, but the same verification requirements apply in these instances.

▶ LEADING-EDGE APPROACH

(see Personal Use Time)

PERSONAL USE TIME

CONSIDER THIS

Many private sector employers are choosing to provide their employees with flexible paid time off instead of sick time, to be used for illness, occasional mental health days, or personal business that cannot be taken care of outside work hours. Offering paid time off in this way would be considered a leading-edge practice.

It is wise to analyze your employees' use of paid sick time, personal days, and vacation time and to determine the budget consequences before choosing to offer flexible paid time off.

▶ CREATIVE APPROACH

(not common; see Floating Personal Days and Sick Time)

▶ BY-THE-BOOK APPROACH

(not common; see Floating Personal Days and Sick Time)

▶ LEADING-EDGE APPROACH

We recognize that we all have responsibilities outside of work. Furthermore, we want to offer our employees some protection against loss of income due to personal or family illness. Therefore, in lieu of sick time, Leading-Edge Agency provides regular employees with personal use time off from work to be used for any of the following:

- Personal illness or injury
- Family illness or injury
- Appointments, routine or otherwise, that cannot be made outside work hours
- Wellness
- Observance of personal, religious, or ethnic holidays not covered by alternative holiday pay

ACCRUAL

All regular staff members who have successfully completed the introductory period will be granted personal use time at the beginning of each fiscal year (prorated on the basis of hire date for the first year of employment):

- Regular full-time staff members: fifteen (15) days per year
- Regular part-time staff members: seven (7) days per year

At the end of each fiscal year, you may donate any unused personal use time to the time share bank (see following section); otherwise, you must forfeit it.

USE

Exempt employees may take personal use time in increments of one (1) day. Nonexempt employees may take personal use time in hourly increments.

We expect all employees to use paid time off responsibly. Employees are asked to schedule personal use time in advance whenever possible. It may be necessary, from time to time, for a manager to request documentation of a personal or family illness. Any employee believed to be abusing paid time off or establishing a pattern of absence that disrupts our services will be subject to disciplinary action up to and including termination. Personal use time cannot be combined with vacation pay except with the advance approval of our human resources director.

Employees do not receive payment for accrued, unused personal use time when they leave Leading-Edge, nor do we offer employees pay in lieu of use while they are with the agency.

PERSONAL TIME SHARE BANK

CONSIDER THIS

CONSIDER THIS

This is an especially appropriate benefit to consider if your nonprofit is involved in health issues, particularly those relating to disabling or life-threatening diseases. However, it is complex to administer and requires a willing accountant or finance department. It is important to funnel donations of earned time off through a "bank" rather than allowing employees to donate time directly to a specific employee, in order to avoid the appearance of favoritism or discrimination in how the benefit is used.

▶ CREATIVE APPROACH

(not common)

▶ BY-THE-BOOK APPROACH

(not common)

▶ LEADING-EDGE APPROACH

At Leading-Edge, we all care about the welfare of our fellow employees. To provide a channel for goodwill and good wishes, we created the Personal Time Share Bank.

The Personal Time Share Bank enables any employee to donate accrued personal use time to colleagues who are experiencing a medical emergency or catastrophic illness that requires substantial time off from work. Any regular employee may donate personal use time, in increments of eight (8) hours, to the Personal Time Share Bank at any time during the year. Forms for this purpose are available from our finance department.

Employees who, due to a medical emergency or catastrophic illness, have used up all their available paid time off and need additional income to supplement state disability income can apply for a grant from the Personal Time Share Bank. Time is granted in eight (8)-hour increments.

The amount of funds available in the Personal Time Share Bank at any given point is determined by the total salary dollars represented by the time donated, not by the actual number of hours donated.

APPLYING FOR PERSONAL TIME SHARE BANK HOURS

Employees may apply for Personal Time Share Bank hours through their manager or a member of the human resources staff. To qualify for a grant, an employee must have exhausted all of his or her available paid time off.

Grants are made on a first-come, first-served basis and are given on the basis of the following criteria:

1. Employees must have regular status and have completed six (6) months of employment.

2. The amount of time in the bank and the number of applicants will determine the time granted to any particular employee.

3. Employees may not have received a previous grant within the past twelve (12)-month period.

TAX CONSEQUENCES

There are no tax consequences to an employee who donates accrued time to the Personal Time Share Bank; the donating employee may not claim the leave as income or as a deductible expense or loss. The employee receiving the donated time, however, does have tax consequences, in that paid time off received by the employee will be considered as income for employment tax purposes.

JURY AND WITNESS DUTY

▶ CREATIVE APPROACH

Both exempt and nonexempt staff members are eligible for up to one (1) week's paid leave when called on to serve as a juror or witness at a trial. You will be asked to provide documentation showing your required days of attendance. If the court releases you after serving a partial day, you are expected to report to work and complete your normal workday unless you make other arrangements with your manager.

Exempt staff members who are required to serve longer than a week and who do some work for Creative Agency during each of the remaining weeks served will continue to receive full pay while on jury duty.

▶ BY-THE-BOOK APPROACH

Regular full-time and regular part-time employees who are called to serve on a jury will be granted up to two (2) weeks' paid leave and will be granted unpaid leave for the remainder of their jury duty. Temporary employees will be granted an unpaid leave for the period of their service. Employees may keep any compensation received in exchange for their jury duty.

Exempt employees who are required to serve longer than two (2) full weeks and who do some work for By-the-Book during each of the remaining weeks that they serve will continue to receive full pay while on jury duty.

Proper documentation demonstrating the required time away from work may be requested prior to granting the leave. If an employee is not required to report or is released early from jury or witness duty, the employee must immediately report to work.

All employees will be granted an unpaid leave if called to serve as a witness in a legal proceeding.

▶ LEADING-EDGE APPROACH

If you receive a proposed juror questionnaire or are called as a witness in a legal proceeding, please notify your manager as soon as possible. If you are called as a juror during a particularly busy time, we may ask you to request the court to postpone your jury duty to a more convenient time.

We will grant regular employees up to twenty (20) days of paid jury duty or witness leave in a calendar year. Court-mandated time beyond twenty (20) days will be unpaid.

Please keep your manager informed of your jury duty or witness status. On days when you serve less than a full day at court, contact your manager to determine whether or not you should return to work. When you return from serving as a juror or witness, you may be required to furnish your manager or our human resources director with appropriate documentation.

Exempt staff members who are required to serve longer than twenty (20) days and who do some work for Leading-Edge during each of the remaining weeks that they serve will continue to receive full pay while on jury duty.

BEREAVEMENT LEAVE

CONSIDER THIS

Demonstrate organizational empathy for employees who have lost close relatives. In addition to paid leave, offer additional unpaid leave, and encourage supervisors to arrange shortened or flexible schedules for employees who are in mourning. It is usually appropriate to send flowers to the funeral or memorial service on behalf of your organization as well.

▶ CREATIVE APPROACH

Bereavement leave allows time for making funeral arrangements and attending the funeral. Staff members who need additional time to attend to the affairs of the deceased or for personal reasons may request to use accrued vacation or sick time or to take time off without pay. Regular staff members receive up to three (3) paid days per occurrence for bereavement leave in cases of a death in the immediate family.

▶ BY-THE-BOOK APPROACH

Regular full- and part-time employees will be granted up to three (3) days of leave, paid at the employee's daily rate of pay, determined by the number of hours the employee is regularly scheduled to work per week, in the event of a death in the employee's immediate family.

▶ LEADING-EDGE APPROACH

Bereavement leave of up to five (5) days with pay is provided to regular full- and part-time employees in the event of a death in the immediate family. You may also seek time off for bereavement leave in the event of the death of a significant person in your life, even if the person is not an immediate family member. We will be as flexible as possible in accommodating these leave requests. Employees seeking paid time off for bereavement leave should communicate with their manager about leave arrangements.

If the cost of a plane ticket would otherwise prevent an employee from attending the funeral of a member of his or her immediate family, Leading-Edge provides limited financial assistance in the form of a no-interest loan for air travel.

TIME OFF TO VOTE

▶ CREATIVE APPROACH

Nonexempt staff members may receive paid time off to vote in city, state, or federal elections. Since polling places are generally open before and after work, we ask that you make every effort to vote outside of your normal working hours. Staff members unable to vote before or after work must make advance arrangements with their manager for reasonable time off to vote at the beginning or end of their normal work hours.

Exempt staff are not paid by the hour, and there will be no salary impact if an exempt staff member takes time to vote during the workday.

▶ BY-THE-BOOK APPROACH

Employees who are unable to vote in an official public election during nonwork hours may arrange, with at least forty-eight (48) hours' advance notice, to take up to two (2) hours off from work, with pay, to vote. Advance approval for such time off must be obtained from the employee's supervisor.

▶ LEADING-EDGE APPROACH

(see policies for the other approaches)

CONSIDER THIS

Many states require you to offer an employee paid time off to vote in any statewide election if the person does not have sufficient time to get to the polls outside of working hours. You also are required to post a notice at least ten (10) days before an election informing employees of their right to this time off.

It's a good idea to apply your policy to all official elections, as it seems rather arbitrary to limit it to statewide elections only.

CHAPTER SIX

Unpaid Time Off and Leaves of Absence

DISABILITY LEAVE

▶ CREATIVE APPROACH

ELIGIBILITY

Full-time and part-time staff members of Creative Agency are eligible for unpaid medical leave after they complete the introductory period (exceptions for pregnancy disability leave may apply). Medical leaves are granted when a staff member is temporarily unable to perform his or her job due to illness, injury, pregnancy, or childbirth. Medical leaves are granted for the duration of the disability, up to a maximum of six (6) months.

REQUESTING A LEAVE

If you become disabled, you should promptly notify your manager. Written certification from your physician or other licensed health practitioner stating the nature of your disability, the date your disability began, and the expected date of your return to work should be provided to your manager. We may request that you provide us with additional medical verification of your continuing disability from time to time during the course of your leave as well.

PAY DURING LEAVE

Staff members must use any accrued sick leave at the beginning of a medical leave. After accrued sick leave is used up, a staff member may use accrued vacation time or apply for state disability benefits or workers' compensation insurance benefits, whichever is appropriate. Staff members are considered inactive when they are no longer being paid and are on a medical leave.

CONSIDER THIS

The laws governing medical leaves of absence are complex and should be closely monitored for changes. Federal law requires employers with fifty or more employees to offer family leave. State laws vary, and many have stricter policies, which you should consult before instigating any disability leave policy.

An employee taking pregnancy disability leave in an organization with fifty or more employees may also be entitled to family leave. Integrating these leaves is complex; if you face this situation as an employer, you may want to consult with an attorney or human resources specialist. (See also Family and Medical Leave.)

RETURN TO WORK

Staff members returning from leaves for pregnancy, childbirth, or other related medical conditions will be guaranteed reemployment in the same position except when, due to organizational necessity, the position has ceased to exist during the leave. In that event, we will seek to provide the returning staff member with a substantially similar position.

Staff members returning from other types of medical leave will be returned to the same or a similar position whenever possible; however, Creative Agency cannot guarantee reemployment.

You may be asked to provide a physician's certification of your fitness to return to work. Your manager should be told in advance of any change in the date of your return to work.

END OF EMPLOYMENT

A staff member away from work on a medical leave will be considered to have voluntarily resigned from Creative Agency in the following circumstances:

- If the staff member fails to notify the agency of his or her availability for work after the disability ceases
- If the staff member fails to return to work after the disability has ceased and a position is available

A staff member who resigns for having exceeded the maximum leave time allowed will be given special rehire consideration when he or she is able to return to work.

Maximum leave time does not apply in cases of work-related illness or injury.

BENEFITS DURING A MEDICAL LEAVE

Creative Agency will continue to provide insurance benefits to staff members during a medical leave, provided that the staff members regularly continue to pay their share of the premium, if applicable.

Benefits that accrue for hours worked will not accrue during a medical leave. Leave time will be counted toward seniority, however.

▶ BY-THE-BOOK APPROACH

MEDICAL DISABILITY LEAVE

Disability leave is available to an employee whose physician certifies that the employee is temporarily disabled from performing his or her job because of illness, injury, physical or mental impairment, pregnancy, or childbirth. After using accrued sick time, an employee may elect to use accrued vacation, provided that the employee gives advance notice of this election to the supervisor prior to or at the time the leave begins. If accrued vacation is to be used, it shall be used at the beginning of the leave or immediately after any accrued sick time is exhausted. Following the use of accrued sick time and vacation time, the remainder of the leave shall be unpaid. Employees on disability leave should apply promptly for state disability insurance, workers' compensation insurance, or long-term disability benefits, whichever is applicable.

Medical certification of disability must be submitted at or before the start of a disability leave of absence and at least every thirty (30) days of leave thereafter, stating the nature of your disability and the expected date of return to work. Requests to extend an initial leave must be accompanied by supporting medical certification and must be received by the supervisor at least two (2) working days in advance of the previously estimated return date. An employee returning to work from a disability leave must give at least two (2) days' advance notice to the supervisor and, upon returning to work, must submit a written release from the employee's physician.

PREGNANCY AND CHILDBIRTH LEAVE

Pregnancy or childbirth leave is not to exceed four (4) months in any twelve (12)-month period and does not have to be continuous. Employees returning from a pregnancy or childbirth leave of absence of four (4) months or less will be returned to the job they left unless, for organizational reasons, By-the-Book was unable to hold the job open or to fill it temporarily because to do so would have resulted in an undue hardship on the agency. Under those circumstances, By-the-Book will offer the employee a substantially similar job if one exists that the employee is qualified to perform.

WORK-RELATED ILLNESS OR INJURY LEAVE

A leave of absence due to a disabling work-related illness or injury is generally not limited in duration. Employees returning from such a leave will be returned to the job they left unless, for organizational reasons, By-the-Book was unable to hold the job open or to fill it temporarily because to do so would have resulted in an undue hardship on the agency. Under those circumstances, By-the-Book will offer the employee a substantially similar job if one exists that the employee is qualified to perform.

NON-WORK-RELATED ILLNESS OR INJURY LEAVE

A leave of absence necessitated by a disabling non-work-related illness, injury, or medical condition that is temporary or of relatively short duration may not exceed two (2) months in any twelve (12)-month period and does not have to be continuous. Employees returning from such a leave of two (2) months or less will be returned to the job they left unless, for organizational reasons, By-the-Book was unable to hold the job opcn or to fill it temporarily because to do so would have resulted in an undue hardship on the agency. Under those circumstances, By-the-Book will offer the employee a substantially similar job if one exists that the employee is qualified to perform.

BENEFITS DURING A MEDICAL LEAVE

By-the-Book will continue to pay for insurance coverage for employees during the unpaid portion of a medical leave up to a maximum of four (4) months. Beyond that time, if additional leave is approved, employees participating in health insurance coverage will be given the option of paying for continued coverage for the duration of the leave.

Benefits that accrue for hours worked will not accrue during a medical leave. Leave time will be counted toward seniority, however.

RESIGNATION DURING A MEDICAL LEAVE

Failure either to comply with By-the-Book's certification and notice requirements during a leave or to return from a leave on the first working day following the end of the leave will be considered a resignation on the part of the employee.

▶ LEADING-EDGE APPROACH

WHO IS ELIGIBLE FOR DISABILITY LEAVE?

A Leading-Edge Agency employee who is temporarily unable to work due to illness, injury, pregnancy, or childbirth may be eligible for an unpaid leave of absence for a period equal to the duration of the disability, up to a maximum of six (6) months in a twelve (12)-month period. If you are temporarily disabled due to a work-related illness or injury, your leave will extend for the duration of your disability or until your disability is determined to be permanent, whichever comes first. Additional information about work-related disability leaves is available from the human resources department.

HOW DO I APPLY FOR DISABILITY LEAVE?

If you become disabled, you should promptly notify your manager. Written certification from your doctor or other licensed health practitioner stating the nature of your disability, the date your disability began, and the expected date of your return to work should be provided to your manager. We may request that you provide us with additional medical verification of your continuing disability from time to time during the course of your leave.

CAN I USE ACCRUED PAID TIME OFF DURING A DISABILITY LEAVE?

We require that you use any accrued personal use time at the beginning of your disability leave. You may then choose to use accrued, unused vacation time or to begin an unpaid leave. You may be eligible to receive state disability insurance benefits, which are administered by the Employment Development Department. Information is available through the EDD and our human resources department.

HOW DOES A DISABILITY LEAVE AFFECT MY JOB?

Employees returning from leaves due to pregnancy, childbirth, or other related medical conditions are guaranteed reemployment unless, for organizational reasons, Leading-Edge was unable to hold the job open or to fill it temporarily because to do so would have resulted in an undue hardship on the agency. If this occurs, Leading-Edge will offer the employee a substantially similar job if one exists that the employee is qualified to perform. Employees returning from other types of disability leave will be returned to the same or a similar position whenever possible; however, Leading-Edge cannot guarantee reemployment.

CAN I RESIGN WHILE ON DISABILITY LEAVE?

A staff member away from work on a medical leave will be considered to have voluntarily resigned from Leading-Edge Agency if he or she gives notice of resignation in writing while on the leave, fails to notify the agency of his or her availability for work after the disability ceases, or fails to return to work after the disability has ceased and a position is available. An employee who resigns for having exceeded the maximum leave time allowed will be given special rehire consideration when he or she is able to return to work. Maximum leave time does not apply in cases of work-related illness or injury.

CAN I COMBINE FAMILY AND MEDICAL LEAVE WITH DISABILITY LEAVE?

An employee may take a maximum of seven (7) months—four (4) months of disability leave plus twelve (12) workweeks—of combined disability and family and medical leave only when she is actually disabled by her pregnancy for four (4) full months and then immediately takes twelve (12) workweeks of baby-bonding family leave.

LONG-TERM ILLNESS OR PERMANENT DISABILITY

▶ ALL APPROACHES

An employee whose leave is necessitated by a disabling non-work-related physical or mental impairment, which substantially limits one of the employee's major life activities and is expected to be ongoing for a substantial period of time or is of permanent duration, may be accommodated with longer and more frequent leaves as long as such leaves will not result in an undue hardship on the agency.

Such employees will be returned to the job they left unless, for organizational reasons, the agency was unable to hold the job open or to fill it temporarily because to do so would have resulted in an undue hardship on the agency. Under those circumstances, the agency will offer the employee a substantially similar job if one exists that the employee is qualified to perform.

⚖ FAMILY AND MEDICAL LEAVE

CONSIDER THIS

Consider using this question-and-answer format to spell out your policy regarding family and medical leave. This format can help employees grasp the many details required of such a policy or locate the answer to a specific question about one aspect of your policy.

▶ CREATIVE APPROACH

(not required for organizations with fewer than fifty employees)

▶ BY-THE-BOOK APPROACH

(not required for organizations with fewer than fifty employees)

▶ LEADING-EDGE APPROACH

An unpaid leave of absence for family or medical care will be granted to all eligible employees for up to twelve (12) weeks in a twelve (12)-month period. The twelve (12)-month period is measured beginning with the month in which the requested leave starts.

WHAT IS FAMILY AND MEDICAL LEAVE?

Family and medical leave is an unpaid leave of up to twelve (12) workweeks in a twelve (12)-month period. The leave is for the birth and care of an employee's newborn child, the placement with the employee of a child for adoption or foster care, or the serious health condition of an employee or an employee's spouse, domestic partner, child, or parent.

WHO CAN TAKE FAMILY AND MEDICAL LEAVE?

An employee is eligible for leave after having worked for Leading-Edge for more than twelve (12) months and for at least 1,250 hours during the twelve (12)-month period immediately prior to the date the leave begins.

WHAT RESTRICTIONS APPLY TO THE WAY LEAVE IS TAKEN?

Leave may be taken intermittently—in two or more blocks of time—or by reducing the employee's normal weekly or daily work schedule. Employees should try to schedule leave in a way that minimizes disruption to the agency's operations.

HOW WILL TAKING FAMILY AND MEDICAL LEAVE AFFECT MY JOB?

Employees who take family and medical leave will return to the same or a comparable position.

WHAT EFFECT WILL FAMILY AND MEDICAL LEAVE HAVE ON MY BENEFITS?

Leading-Edge will maintain existing benefits coverage during the leave period. Employees are required to continue copayments (when applicable) during the leave.

A family and medical leave will not be considered working time for the purposes of accrual of vacation and health and wellness leave.

CAN I USE ACCRUED PAID TIME OFF DURING THIS LEAVE?

Employees are required to apply any accrued paid time off (vacation, health and wellness) toward family and medical leave.

HOW MUCH NOTICE MUST I GIVE BEFORE TAKING FAMILY AND MEDICAL LEAVE?

Employees are required to provide thirty (30) days' advance notice of the need to take leave when the need is foreseeable and such notice is possible. Thirty (30) days prior to taking the leave or, if less, as soon as the need for a leave is known, employees should inform both their manager and the human resources director of their intention to take the leave.

CAN FAMILY AND MEDICAL LEAVE BE DENIED?

In certain circumstances, an employee may be denied a leave if it will cause substantial and grievous economic injury to Leading-Edge Agency.

SCHOOL LEAVE

▶ CREATIVE APPROACH

Staff members with responsibility for school-age children may take up to forty (40) hours of unpaid leave per calendar year to attend school functions or meet with teachers.

▶ BY-THE-BOOK APPROACH

An employee who is the parent, guardian, or custodial grandparent of a school-age child may take up to forty (40) hours of leave per school year for the purpose of participating in the child's school activities or to discuss the child's possible suspension. In taking such leave, employees may take unpaid time off or use accrued vacation time. School-related leaves cannot exceed eight (8) hours in any calendar month.

Employees who take school-related leave must make arrangements for the time off with their supervisor as soon as the need for the leave is known. By-the-Book may request written documentation from the school reflecting the date and time of the activity attended.

No discriminatory action will be taken against any employee for taking school-related time off.

▶ LEADING-EDGE APPROACH

We encourage our employees with school-age children to be involved with their children's education. To facilitate school involvement, we provide all employees with up to sixteen (16) hours of paid time off per year to participate in school-related activities or to meet with teachers or school administrators.

Beyond paid time off, employees may take an additional twenty-four (24) hours of unpaid leave for school-related activities during the school year. Employees may apply accrued personal time to school-related time off. We do ask that you take no more than eight (8) hours per month of school-related time off.

Employees must make arrangements for taking school-related time off with their manager as far in advance as possible. Your manager may request that you provide documentation of a particular school activity or event.

DRUG OR ALCOHOL REHABILITATION LEAVE

▶ CREATIVE APPROACH

(not legally required in small organizations)

▶ BY-THE-BOOK APPROACH

By-the-Book Agency recognizes that drug and alcohol abuse are serious medical problems and wants to assist employees who realize that they have such a problem, which may interfere with their ability to perform their job in a satisfactory manner. Employees who decide to enroll voluntarily in a rehabilitation program due to a problem with drugs or alcohol use will be given time off to participate in such a program, and By-the-Book will make reasonable efforts to keep this fact confidential.

To be granted a leave for this purpose, the employee must submit certification of enrollment in a drug or alcohol rehabilitation program at or before the leave begins. The certification must include a statement that the employee's participation in the program prevents him or her from working and must specify beginning and ending dates of the program and the employee's estimated date of return to work. An extension of the leave requires supporting documentation prior to the end of the initial leave.

Employees returning from such a leave will be returned to the job they left unless, for organizational reasons, By-the-Book was unable to hold the job open or to fill it temporarily because to do so would have resulted in an undue hardship on the agency. Under those circumstances, By-the-Book will offer the employee a substantially similar job if one exists that the employee is qualified to perform.

▶ LEADING-EDGE APPROACH

(see By-the-Book Approach)

CONSIDER THIS

Laws regarding drug or alcohol rehabilitation leave vary by state and should be consulted before implementing any policy. In some states, employers of twenty-five (25) or more employees must reasonably accommodate an employee who wants to participate in an alcohol or drug rehabilitation program. However, these laws do not protect from disciplinary action or termination an employee whose job performance is hampered significantly by drug or alcohol use. (See also Employee Assistance Program in Chapter Four.)

MILITARY LEAVE

CONSIDER THIS

Federal law requires employers to treat reservists and members of the National Guard who are deployed into active service and employees who are drafted into service as you would any other employee on a protected leave. This means that you must reinstate them to the same or a similar position with the same seniority, benefits, and pay as when they left.

Employers are not required to continue to pay an employee on military leave.

▶ CREATIVE APPROACH

We seek to comply with all state and federal laws regarding leaves of absence for military duty. Please speak with your office manager or the executive director in the event that you need to schedule such a leave.

▶ BY-THE-BOOK APPROACH

Employees who are or who become members of the National Guard or military reserves will be granted a leave of absence to attend military training in either mandatory or voluntary status for a maximum period of fifteen (15) calendar days annually. By-the-Book will cover the difference between an employee's regular pay for the period and the pay received from the military when training is mandatory. Such pay will not be provided to cover lost earnings in the case of voluntary training.

Employees who leave our employ for active military duty, active duty for training, initial active duty for training, inactive duty training, full-time National Guard duty, or examinations to determine fitness for duty in any branch of the armed forces of the United States will be reinstated with accrued tenure (including seniority and accrued benefits). This is in accordance with the provisions of the Uniformed Services Employment and Reemployment Rights Act of 1994.

Employees must advise their supervisors of their military training schedule as far in advance as possible.

▶ LEADING-EDGE APPROACH

If you are a member of the National Guard or military reserves and are directed to participate in periodic field training, you will receive unpaid military leave for a maximum period of fifteen (15) calendar days a year. Such leave will have no impact on your regular vacation accrual. If you have some choice as to when to attend yearly training, we ask that you select a period that will be convenient for the organization and for your coworkers.

Employees who are indefinitely deployed in active service via the draft or by order of the president of the United States are entitled to military leave. Such military leave is without pay and ends either ninety (90) days after an employee's discharge from the service or one (1) year after the employee is released from hospitalization continuing after discharge. The employee will be reinstated to his or her former position or to a position of similar seniority, status, and pay if the agency is informed of the discharge no fewer than sixty (60) days prior to the employee's planned return to work.

PERSONAL LEAVE

CONSIDER THIS

Although you are not required by law to provide any unpaid personal leave time, you are more likely to retain dedicated employees if you provide them with some flexibility to deal with life's unexpected crises and opportunities.

As with any leave policy, be sure you spell out who is eligible, the maximum length of the leave, and whether or not you will provide benefits coverage during the leave.

▶ CREATIVE APPROACH

We have a policy of granting a personal leave of absence in exceptional cases when time away from work will allow a staff member to deal with an unexpected and serious personal situation. A personal leave of absence may be granted for up to a maximum of thirty (30) workdays.

A personal leave will not be considered an interruption of service for benefits purposes; however, no benefits based on time worked will accrue during such a leave. If you feel you need a personal leave, you should discuss your circumstances with your manager.

If you do not return from a personal leave on or before the last day of the leave, you may be considered to have resigned from Creative Agency.

▶ BY-THE-BOOK APPROACH

Employees are expected to maintain a continuous record of employment. However, we recognize that it may be necessary for an employee to be excused from work for personal reasons. In such cases, employees must submit a request for a personal leave of absence as far in advance as possible. All requests will be given every consideration consistent with the urgency and need of the employee's circumstances, the employee's job performance, and the department's workload. Authorization for such personal leaves of absence is fully at the discretion of the executive director.

Personal leaves of absence are without pay and are available to full- and part-time employees who have completed one (1) year of service. Failing to return to work upon completion of the leave or working for another employer during the leave without prior approval will be considered a resignation.

A personal leave of absence of no more than thirty (30) days will not be considered an interruption of continuous service with respect to benefit plans. Employees on personal leaves of more than thirty (30) days may continue insurance coverage by paying the cost of the monthly premium. Benefits that normally accrue for hours worked will not accrue during a leave. Upon returning from a personal leave, an employee will have the same amount of seniority as when the leave began. All personal leaves are granted at the discretion of management, based on our needs related to your position and the hardship that might result from your absence at a particular time.

▶ LEADING-EDGE APPROACH

Occasionally, employees face compelling personal needs that may require them to take time off from work. Leading-Edge Agency would prefer that an employee request a personal leave of absence rather than resign. This allows us the possibility of working through the situation rather than losing a valued employee.

To be eligible for a personal leave, you must have completed at least one (1) year of continuous employment and have received a satisfactory performance evaluation. All personal leaves are granted at the discretion of management, based on our needs related to your position and the hardship that might result from your absence at a particular time.

If granted, personal leaves cannot exceed ninety (90) days. These leaves are unpaid, although Leading-Edge will continue to provide health benefits coverage for the duration of the leave. Employees on personal leave do not accumulate service time but keep their existing seniority upon return to active status.

Failure to return to work immediately following the leave of absence is regarded as a voluntary resignation.

SABBATICAL LEAVE

▶ CREATIVE APPROACH

(not common)

▶ BY-THE-BOOK APPROACH

(not common)

▶ LEADING-EDGE APPROACH

To encourage employees periodically to step back from the day-to-day concerns and pressures of our work, we offer a six (6)-week unpaid sabbatical leave to all regular full-and part-time employees. To be eligible for sabbatical leave, employees must complete five (5) years of continuous service and have a satisfactory job performance rating as evidenced by the two most recent evaluations at the time the leave is requested.

Sabbatical leave requires the approval of the executive director and must be arranged at least three (3) months in advance. Employees returning from sabbatical leave will be reinstated to the same or a substantially similar position. Although benefits do not accrue during sabbatical leave, Leading-Edge will continue to pay for health insurance coverage during the leave.

Eligible employees may apply for sabbatical leave once every five (5) years.

PART FOUR

Developing Fair, Straightforward Policies for Workplace Standards and Practices

CHAPTER SEVEN

Work Hours and Pay

WORKWEEK

▶ CREATIVE APPROACH

Our workweeks are Sunday through Saturday.

▶ BY-THE-BOOK APPROACH

The workweek commences at 12:01 a.m. Monday and ends at midnight Sunday. The standard workweek for a full-time employee is 37.5 hours.

▶ LEADING-EDGE APPROACH

(see policies for the other approaches)

CONSIDER THIS

It is important to define your workweek if you have a large number of hourly, nonexempt employees, particularly if they work flexible schedules or weekends. This prevents confusion about the specific number of hours or days represented on a single paycheck.

PAY PERIODS

CONSIDER THIS

You are legally required to post your payday schedule where it will be visible to all employees.

▶ CREATIVE APPROACH

We pay staff members twice a month. Payday is the 10th and the 25th day of the month, unless that payday falls on a holiday or weekend. In that case, staff members will be paid on the last working day before the holiday or weekend.

▶ BY-THE-BOOK APPROACH

For all employees, the standard pay period is semimonthly (15th and last working day of the month). When a payday falls on a weekend or holiday, paychecks will be distributed on the last working day prior to the weekend or holiday.

▶ LEADING-EDGE APPROACH

You are paid every other Friday for work completed through the previous Saturday. Our payroll and holiday schedules are distributed annually.

WORK SCHEDULES

▶ CREATIVE APPROACH

Creative Agency's offices are normally open to the public, volunteers, and visitors Monday through Friday from 9:00 a.m. to 5:00 p.m. Although the majority of our staff members work those hours, some may work alternative schedules based on arrangements with their manager.

Nonexempt staff members should not start work before their scheduled start time or work beyond their accustomed ending time without the prior approval of their manager.

▶ BY-THE-BOOK APPROACH

Employees of By-the-Book Agency are expected to work the number of hours agreed on at the time of hire.

Although the regular workweek is from 9:00 a.m. to 5:00 p.m. Monday through Friday, other work arrangements may be made between the employee and his or her supervisor, subject to the demands and limitations of the job and department. Supervisors have final approval for flextime requests and retain the authority to require the employee to return to a regular schedule should organizational need require it.

▶ LEADING-EDGE APPROACH

Work schedules at Leading-Edge Agency are based on department or facility functions and individual job responsibilities. Work schedules may vary from department to department and employee to employee. All schedules are subject to change and require a manager's approval.

Full-time employees are expected to work an average of forty (40) hours per week.

FLEXTIME

We recognize that we can accomplish our organizational goals and support employees' family and personal responsibilities by making it possible for you to work a schedule that does not conform to

---

CONSIDER THIS

Employers should try to be as flexible as possible with work schedules. However, you should have a policy stating that you reserve the right to request a change in work schedule to avoid complications resulting from too many different scheduling needs.

If you are considering creating an alternative work schedule for full-time employees, such as a workweek of four ten-hour days, you should closely follow state wage and hour law requirements for establishing such a schedule. For example, you may be required to hold a vote of all eligible employees to determine if a majority wish to switch to a flextime schedule.

our regular hours of operation. We encourage you to use flextime when it can accommodate both personal and agency needs. Flextime requirements are as follows:

- Work must be suitable to flextime scheduling.
- The flextime schedule will not inconvenience coworkers.
- You have your manager's approval.

MEAL AND REST PERIODS

▶ CREATIVE APPROACH

All nonexempt staff members receive a paid ten (10)-minute rest period for each four (4) hours worked or major fraction thereof. Full-time staff members should take one rest period in the first half of their day and one in the second half.

Nonexempt staff members who work five (5) hours or more receive an unpaid lunch break of thirty (30) minutes. Rest periods cannot be combined with the lunch break, but staff members may take up to a one (1)-hour lunch break if desired. Staff members may not skip rest and meal breaks to shorten the workday.

▶ BY-THE-BOOK APPROACH

(see Creative Approach)

▶ LEADING-EDGE APPROACH

We maintain an informal atmosphere and do not have a formal system for scheduling breaks during the workday. All employees are encouraged to pause during the workday to rest and give the eyes, hands, mouth, and ears a break.

Nonexempt employees are required to take a paid fifteen (15)-minute break during each four (4)-hour block of work. Nonexempt employees must also take a half-hour paid lunch break and have the option of taking an additional unpaid half-hour.

We ask that all employees coordinate lunch and rest breaks with coworkers to ensure adequate coverage for all functions.

If you are nonexempt (entitled to overtime pay), you may not skip your breaks or meal period, nor can you combine breaks with lunch. It's the law!

CONSIDER THIS

Most state laws do not allow a nonexempt employee to combine paid breaks with a lunch hour or to skip breaks in order to leave earlier in the day. You are not required to pay nonexempt employees for lunch breaks, although some nonprofits choose to do so.

Nonexempt employees who are required to do any work (such as answering phones or remaining in the office) during their lunch break must be paid for this time.

TIMEKEEPING REQUIREMENTS

▶ CREATIVE APPROACH

All staff members must complete a time sheet for each pay period. Nonexempt staff members should record actual hours worked plus all use of paid time off. Exempt staff members need only track use of paid days off.

▶ BY-THE-BOOK APPROACH

All employees submit time sheets for each pay period. Nonexempt employees record actual hours worked and leave taken, and exempt employees record leave taken. Any falsification of a time sheet will result in disciplinary action, up to and including discharge.

▶ LEADING-EDGE APPROACH

(see policies for the other approaches; this type of policy is very straightforward)

OVERTIME PAY

▶ CREATIVE APPROACH

Overtime is paid to nonexempt staff members according to federal and state law. Exempt staff members are not eligible for overtime pay. Overtime hours must be approved in advance by your manager.

Only hours actually worked are used to compute overtime earnings. Paid time off, such as holidays or vacation time, is not used to compute overtime.

▶ BY-THE-BOOK APPROACH

(see Leading-Edge Approach policy)

▶ LEADING-EDGE APPROACH

Nonexempt employees are paid at the rate of one and one-half (1.5) times their regular rate of pay for hours worked in excess of forty (40) in a workweek.

Overtime is not at the employee's discretion; it requires advance supervisory approval. Leading-Edge Agency does not provide compensatory time off as a substitute for overtime pay. Vacation, holiday, and sick time do not constitute hours worked for the purposes of computing overtime.

Ordinarily, exempt employees are not compensated for working more than forty (40) hours in a week. In unusual circumstances, when an exempt employee is required to work a substantial number of extra hours, the supervisor may grant compensatory paid time off. Such time must be taken within thirty (30) days of the extra time worked.

SALARY ADVANCES

CONSIDER THIS

Many organizations choose not to allow employee salary advances at all because some employees can become habitual "borrowers." If you do allow salary advances, define the circumstances for an advance very narrowly, such as in the accompanying policy.

▶ ALL APPROACHES

A salary advance can be given when a staff member is scheduled to take a vacation, up to the amount already accrued and scheduled for use during the vacation.

A salary advance for any other reason requires approval of the executive director and will be granted only in emergency situations. Any staff member receiving a salary advance (other than for vacation) must pay back the entire advance through payroll deductions within thirty (30) days of receiving the advance.

Salary advances for any reason are limited to three (3) per calendar year.

WAGE GARNISHMENTS

▶ ALL APPROACHES

From time to time, we may be required to withhold monies from an employee's pay. If this agency receives a court-authorized garnishment or levy, the staff member affected will be notified immediately.

PAYROLL DEDUCTIONS

CONSIDER THIS

It is helpful to include this type of policy statement in your handbook because many employees are confused by the bite taken out of their paycheck by mandatory deductions. It's also a good idea to identify someone in your organization with whom employees can discuss their options for voluntary deductions and the impact of deductions on their take-home pay.

▶ CREATIVE APPROACH

Your payroll and earnings deductions are detailed with your check. Mandated and voluntary deductions usually include the following:

Deductions Mandated by Federal and State Law	Voluntary Deductions
Federal income tax	Health insurance
State income tax	Flexible spending account
Social Security, Medicare contributions	Savings
State disability insurance	Repayment of salary advances
Workers' compensation insurance	United Way contributions
Garnishments, wage attachments	Federal unemployment insurance

Any questions about your paycheck should be directed to the director of finance.

▶ BY-THE-BOOK APPROACH

(same as Creative Approach policy)

▶ LEADING-EDGE APPROACH

Attached to your paycheck is a stub showing the number of hours you worked during the pay period, the amount of your total earnings, specific contributions to benefit plans, and the amounts of specific deductions as required by law or authorized by you. We suggest that you review your pay stub carefully each pay period and that you retain it for your records. If you have any questions about your deductions, please contact the payroll coordinator in our finance department.

SALARY PHILOSOPHY

▶ CREATIVE APPROACH

At Creative Agency, we strive for fairness and equity in all our policies and practices, including those that affect compensation. We offer a compensation package (your annual salary plus benefits) that reflects competitiveness in the marketplace and concern for our staff members' ability to balance their work and personal lives.

▶ BY-THE-BOOK APPROACH

It is the policy of By-the-Book Agency to make every effort to compensate employees fairly and equitably and to recognize the contributions made by existing employees as its highest priority in budgeting expenses.

The board of directors sets the salary of the executive director. The executive director sets all other salaries according to ranges approved by the board. Periodically, the executive director reviews salaries for all positions and uses information about compensation at other agencies to ensure that By-the-Book remains competitive in its compensation practices.

▶ LEADING-EDGE APPROACH

It is important to us, as leaders in our community, that our compensation levels reflect the outstanding capabilities of our employees. The primary objective of our compensation program is to encourage and reinforce the attraction and retention of talented and dedicated employees.

Compensation ranges are reviewed annually and are designed to reflect competitiveness and equity based on internal and external factors. If you have questions or concerns about your salary level, you are encouraged to speak frankly with your manager or to meet with a member of our human resources staff.

CONSIDER THIS

It is beyond the scope of this handbook to cover salary administration policies and practices, but these are reviewed in depth in The Management Center's *Nonprofit Guide to Developing and Administering Sound Compensation Policies,* which has been designed as a companion volume to this handbook.

SALARY REVIEWS

CONSIDER THIS

More and more nonprofit organizations are moving away from automatic salary increases and are instead offering performance-linked increases. If your organization is considering a change to performance-based pay, I recommend that you consult with a qualified compensation specialist about the many options available to you.

If yours is a large organization with opportunities for promotion and internal transfers, it is helpful to have a policy that stipulates how a promotional pay increase will affect an employee's annual salary review. If salary reviews are done on an anniversary-of-hire basis, a midyear promotion should change the salary review date.

▶ CREATIVE APPROACH

Staff members have the opportunity for a salary increase annually at the time of their anniversary of hire or twelve (12) months from their most recent salary review. Increases are not automatic but are based on overall job performance and agency budget. Staff members who are on written warning are not eligible for salary increases until their performance or other job-related issues are satisfactorily resolved.

▶ BY-THE-BOOK APPROACH

(same as Creative Approach policy)

▶ LEADING-EDGE APPROACH

All employees receive a compensation review as part of their annual performance evaluation process, which takes place at the end of the fiscal year. To be eligible for an increase, employees must have been employed for at least six (6) months; increases given after more or less than twelve (12) months of employment are prorated.

Leading-Edge Agency grants salary increases on the basis of job performance, and increases are never guaranteed. Our pay-for-performance program is designed as an incentive to reward outstanding job performance. We consider the following factors when determining a performance-based salary increase:

- Budget available for increases. Guidelines for salary increases are issued annually to reflect current budget capabilities.
- Employee's overall job performance over the previous twelve (12) months.
- Performance of employee's entire department or work group in meeting annual objectives.
- Employee's salary in relation to comparable salaries in like positions inside the organization.
- Changes in the cost of living.

In addition, you may receive a salary increase if you are promoted or given substantially new responsibilities or if it is determined that your salary level is not equitable in comparison with that of others in like positions with similar levels of seniority.

CHAPTER EIGHT

Workplace Health and Safety

SAFETY POLICY

▶ CREATIVE APPROACH

Creative Agency expects its staff members to work in a safe manner, to use good judgment and common sense in matters of safety, to observe all safety rules published and posted in various areas, and to follow all federal and state OSHA regulations. At the time of hire, all new staff members receive a safety orientation, including training on disaster preparedness. If you have any questions or concerns about workplace safety, or if you would like to review our complete safety program, please speak with your office manager.

▶ BY-THE-BOOK APPROACH

By-the-Book Agency strives to provide a safe and healthful workplace and to prevent accidental injury through employee training and education. The agency maintains a safety manual with complete information on all aspects of our safety program.

By-the-Book's managers and supervisors are responsible for overseeing the safety programs of the organization. All supervisors are required to see that every employee has read the safety rules. Furthermore, supervisors are expected to enforce all safety rules as the surest method of preventing accidents and injuries.

It is the responsibility of the director of operations to oversee proper care, storage, and maintenance of all equipment and potentially hazardous materials (including chemicals such as toner or cleaning agents). The operations staff regularly conducts safety reviews of work areas and takes steps to correct any potentially hazardous situations.

All employees and volunteers are required to work in a safe and responsible manner. Safety requirements for employees and volunteers include all of the following:

- Considering safety as a daily on-the-job priority
- Following all safety rules and work procedures
- Immediately reporting any unsafe condition, accident, or near-miss to their supervisor

CONSIDER THIS

All employers, regardless of the size of their staff, should emphasize the importance of safety on the job. A handbook is a good place to state some general policies about workplace safety and health. This type of general policy statement does not fulfill the requirements for compliance with many state laws, which require all employers to prepare and implement an illness and injury prevention program, the details of which are beyond the scope of this handbook. Chambers of commerce have many health and safety publications, the contents of which are applicable to nonprofit employers. (See also Workers' Compensation in Chapter Four.)

- Maintaining a clean and orderly work area
- Working only with equipment or materials with which they are familiar and for which they've been properly trained
- Always wearing seat belts when traveling on agency business

Any willful violation of a safety procedure can result in immediate termination of employment.

▶ LEADING-EDGE APPROACH

Leading-Edge Agency strives to provide each of our employees and volunteers with a safe, comfortable, and healthy work environment.

We provide all employees with the tools, training, facilities, and information necessary to work in a safe and efficient manner. We ask you to approach your work with a thoughtfulness that reflects your respect for your own health and safety and that of your fellow employees.

Leading-Edge strives to comply with all workplace safety laws and regulations; employees are responsible for taking the opportunities provided to understand them and observe them. Our fundamental belief is that no one task is so important that it warrants risking the health or safety of any employee at any time. Safety and emergency procedure information is available from the safety coordinator in your department or from your manager.

If you have any questions or concerns about workplace health or safety, please speak to your manager or any member of our human resources staff. Any employee who wishes at any time to report an unsafe or hazardous workplace situation may do so anonymously by placing a call to our safety hot line at STA-SAFE.

DRUG-FREE WORKPLACE

▶ CREATIVE APPROACH

All staff members are expected to understand and comply with the following guidelines regarding the use of drugs or alcohol in the workplace:

1. We prohibit the unlawful use, possession, distribution, sale, or manufacture of a controlled substance on our premises.

2. We prohibit all staff members from being under the influence of drugs or alcohol while on the job. Exceptions for medicines are made on a case-by-case basis.

3. Failure to follow Creative Agency's drug-free workplace policy may result in disciplinary action including suspension without pay, mandatory participation in a drug rehabilitation program on the first offense, and termination on the second.

4. If you are convicted of violating any criminal drug statute in the workplace, you are required to notify the executive director within five (5) calendar days of the conviction.

▶ BY-THE-BOOK APPROACH

As part of By-the-Book's ongoing commitment to a safe and healthy workplace, we maintain a drug-free workplace policy. Any employee who reports to work while under the influence of drugs or alcohol runs the risks of endangering his or her safety and the safety of others, destruction of or damage to personal or agency property, and a loss of productivity and workplace morale.

All employees and volunteers of By-the-Book are required to understand and comply with the agency's drug-free workplace policy. Any failure to comply with the guidelines of this policy can result in immediate termination of employment. Employees and volunteers either in our offices or conducting business on behalf of our agency regardless of location are prohibited from all of the following:

CONSIDER THIS

The federal Drug-Free Workplace Act of 1988 applies to all employers who receive grants of any size from the federal government and to contractors who do $25,000 or more in business with the federal government. Many states have adopted similar statutes, and these should be consulted before instigating any personnel policies. If you determine that you are required to follow the federal or state requirements for a drug-free workplace, you should consult with your labor attorney or review a labor law publication to learn what you need to do to be in compliance.

Many nonprofit employers choose to institute a strict antidrug policy, even when they are not required by the terms of state or federal grants.

- Unauthorized use, possession, purchase, sale, manufacture, distribution, transportation, or dispensation of any controlled substance.

- Reporting to work while under the influence of alcohol or a controlled substance. Controlled substances include, but are not limited to, narcotics (such as heroin and morphine), cannabis (marijuana, hashish), stimulants (such as cocaine and amphetamines), depressants (tranquilizers) except by doctor's prescription, and hallucinogens (such as PCP, LSD, and "designer drugs").

- Use, possession, purchase, sale, manufacture, distribution, transportation, or dispensation of any legal prescription drug in an illegal manner.

- Reporting to work while impaired by the use of a legal drug whenever such impairment might substantially interfere with job performance, pose a threat to the employee's safety or the safety of others, or risk significant damage to agency property.

CONVICTION NOTIFICATION

An employee who is convicted of violating a criminal drug statute in the workplace must inform the executive director or operations director of this agency (including pleas of guilty or nolo contendere) within five (5) days of the conviction. Failure to so inform the agency will result in disciplinary action up to and including termination of employment.

SUBSTANCE ABUSE EDUCATION AND TREATMENT

By-the-Book offers regular training to supervisors to assist in identifying and addressing substance abuse on the job. In addition, the agency periodically offers an education program for all employees on the dangers of substance abuse in the workplace.

For employees who seek help in overcoming drug and alcohol abuse problems, By-the-Book Agency offers both medical benefits for substance abuse treatment and information about community resources for treatment. An employee who voluntarily enters a substance abuse treatment program will not be penalized or discriminated against in any way by the agency.

Employees who violate the drug-free workplace policy may, at the discretion of management, be required to attend a rehabilitation or drug abuse assistance program as an alternative to disciplinary action. Employees given this opportunity must satisfactorily participate in the program as a condition of continued employment.

▶ LEADING-EDGE APPROACH

(see policies for the other approaches)

SMOKING

CONSIDER THIS

Many state laws require that employers must prohibit smoking in any enclosed area of the workplace. To prevent secondhand-smoke wars, it is helpful to designate places where employees may smoke if you have a large number of smokers and operate in your own separate facility.

▶ CREATIVE APPROACH

In consideration of the health and safety of all our staff members, we maintain a smoke-free environment.

▶ BY-THE-BOOK APPROACH

Smoking is prohibited in all By-the-Book offices.

▶ LEADING-EDGE APPROACH

Smoking is not permitted in any Leading-Edge facility. If you smoke, please demonstrate consideration for your fellow employees when you choose an outside smoking location.

Leading-Edge encourages our employees who smoke to quit. If you are interested in the smoking cessation program offered through our health maintenance organization, please contact our benefits administrator in human resources.

USE OF PERSONAL FRAGRANCE

▶ LEADING-EDGE APPROACH

Some of our employees are highly sensitive to perfumes, colognes, and other personal fragrances. We ask that you consider the sensitivities of others before you choose to wear fragrances at work. Any employee who is experiencing a problem with fragrances worn by a fellow employee is encouraged to ask, respectfully, that the work area be kept fragrance-free.

CONSIDER THIS

A policy that addresses this issue is becoming increasingly popular as individuals with a sensitivity to fragrances are becoming more vocal

CHAPTER NINE

Work Practices and Environment

AIDS AND OTHER LIFE-THREATENING ILLNESSES

▶ LEADING-EDGE APPROACH

At Leading-Edge, we believe that employees with life-threatening illnesses (including, but not limited to cancer, HIV or AIDS, heart disease, and multiple sclerosis) should continue to work for as long as their condition allows them to do so in a safe and satisfactory manner.

We believe that a supportive and caring work environment is an important factor in maintaining quality of life for an employee with a life-threatening illness. We ask all our employees to be sensitive to the needs of colleagues facing such an illness. Managers should provide ill employees with referrals to available services and assist them with personal support appropriate to the work environment.

Upon request, Leading-Edge will provide reasonable accommodation to employees with a life-threatening illness to enable them to continue to work. This might include flexible schedules to accommodate medical treatments and tasks that do not require physical exertion. Through continuing education and communication, we will attempt to create a supportive, open, and informed work environment in which anyone with a life-threatening illness will feel free to come forward in the knowledge that he or she will be met with respect, understanding, and care.

An employee with a life-threatening illness is under no obligation to disclose that condition to the agency. If an employee chooses to discuss a life-threatening illness, any such conversation will be considered strictly confidential and will not be disclosed to others without the employee's permission (except as required by law). Unauthorized disclosure of confidential information relating to health status will lead to disciplinary action, up to and including dismissal.

Employees with AIDS or HIV are entitled to the full range of medical insurance and disability benefits provided for employees with life-threatening illnesses.

PUNCTUALITY AND ATTENDANCE

CONSIDER THIS

When crafting a policy about punctuality and attendance, it is important to be very specific about notification. Spell out exactly when an employee is expected to notify his or her supervisor of lateness or absence so that your agency can avoid a mad scramble for coverage.

▶ CREATIVE APPROACH

We expect staff members to arrive at work on time and to work their full weekly schedule. If you need to be absent from work for any reason, you must call your supervisor before the start of your workday—ideally, the night before.

▶ BY-THE-BOOK APPROACH

Employees who are unable to report for work for any reason must notify their immediate supervisor within one (1) hour of their regularly scheduled starting time.

In general, all employees are expected to be responsible and demonstrate respect for fellow employees by establishing a record of punctuality and regular attendance. These are factors considered in evaluating overall job performance.

Frequent lateness or excessive absenteeism may result in disciplinary action up to and including termination.

▶ LEADING-EDGE APPROACH

(see policies for the other approaches)

USE OF FACILITIES AND PROPERTY

▶ CREATIVE APPROACH

We ask that you exercise care when using Creative Agency property and equipment. If you find that office equipment is damaged or malfunctioning, please let our executive director know about it immediately.

▶ BY-THE-BOOK APPROACH

Employees are asked to treat agency property as they would their own. Specifically, employees are to keep their own work area and common areas clean and well maintained and limit their use of agency equipment to work-related purposes. Employees are required to receive supervisory approval before removing any agency property from the premises.

Occasionally, employees may need to enter agency premises after the offices are closed to retrieve personal items or to complete projects. Employees must provide their supervisor with advance notice if they intend to enter the premises after office hours.

▶ LEADING-EDGE APPROACH

(see policies for the other approaches)

CONSIDER THIS

It is wise to spell out a general policy about the use of agency facilities and property. The larger the organization, the greater the risk that occasionally an employee may decide that one computer or other piece of equipment "won't be missed." A stated policy provides a basis for disciplinary action for unauthorized "borrowing" or use of agency equipment and facilities.

GUESTS AND VISITORS

CONSIDER THIS

Include this type of policy in your handbook if you have a problem with excessive visitors in your offices or if the work is such that a high level of privacy must be maintained. Generally, employees exercise good judgment about workplace visitors, so a written policy can seem unduly harsh unless clearly warranted by circumstances.

▶ CREATIVE APPROACH

(not common in small organizations)

▶ BY-THE-BOOK APPROACH

Employees are asked to keep on-the-job visitors to a minimum to ensure that the workplace is not unduly interrupted. All visitors should remain in the reception area until escorted by the appropriate employee.

▶ LEADING-EDGE APPROACH

Please keep visits from friends and family to a minimum, in order to preserve an appropriate work environment. We provide a number of opportunities throughout the year for friends and family to visit our workplace, and visits are best made during those times.

SECURITY

▶ CREATIVE APPROACH

(not common in small organizations)

▶ BY-THE-BOOK APPROACH

(same as Leading-Edge Approach policy)

▶ LEADING-EDGE APPROACH

Leading-Edge strives to provide a secure work environment for our employees, volunteers, clients, and visitors. We provide for the security of our buildings and facilities by maintaining alarms and outside security services. We ask that you comply with all security procedures established in your work area and that you immediately report any breach of security to your manager.

We encourage employees to be prudent about bringing personal items to work. Leading-Edge is not responsible for losses resulting from theft of property while you are away from your work area.

Immediately report lost or stolen keys or missing agency property to your supervisor. Copying or giving keys or lock combinations to an unauthorized individual will be considered grounds for immediate dismissal.

CONSIDER THIS

A security policy does not take the place of security measures and procedures. Depending on your organization's location and facilities, you may want to provide specific training on security procedures.

PERSONAL USE OF PHONES

▶ CREATIVE APPROACH

Although occasional personal phone calls are to be expected, please confine your use of the phones to agency business as much as possible. Should circumstances require that you place a long-distance call, we ask that you use a personal calling card or call collect.

▶ BY-THE-BOOK APPROACH

(same as the Creative Approach policy)

▶ LEADING-EDGE APPROACH

The telephone is one of our most important service tools. Please be certain that your phone manner reflects care and courtesy toward our clients and the public. Except in cases of emergency, please keep personal phone calls brief and infrequent.

USE OF PERSONAL AUTOMOBILE

▶ ALL APPROACHES

Employees who use their own automobiles for travel on authorized agency business will be reimbursed for mileage at the rate established by the Internal Revenue Service. Employees must have prior supervisory approval for the use of personal vehicles and must carry, at their own expense, the minimum insurance coverage for property damage and public liability.

CONSIDER THIS

If your employees use their own vehicles to conduct agency business or to commute between work locations, you should clearly spell out your reimbursement and insurance policies. In general, it is best to avoid relying on employee vehicles for jobs that require a substantial amount of driving because owning or leasing vehicles will be less expensive for the agency in the long run.

ATTIRE AND
PERSONAL HYGIENE

▶ ALL APPROACHES

It is expected that employees will maintain a clean and neat appearance and will project a professional and businesslike image in dealing with other employees, clients, volunteers, and the general public. The agency reserves the right to define appropriate standards of appearance for the workplace.

EXPENSE REIMBURSEMENT

▶ CREATIVE APPROACH

Staff members are reimbursed for approved travel and entertainment expenses. Staff members are asked to complete a record of all expenses for which they seek reimbursement and to submit receipts along with the expense record for reimbursement. Reimbursement is made via check within two (2) weeks of receipt of the reimbursement request.

▶ BY-THE-BOOK APPROACH

Reasonable and customary personal expenses incurred in the performance of one's job will be reimbursed. Reimbursement requires prior authorization by the employee's immediate supervisor, approval of actual expenses, and completion of a signed, itemized voucher.

▶ LEADING-EDGE APPROACH

(see policies for the other approaches)

CONSIDER THIS

Keep situations requiring employees to pay work-related expenses to a minimum. Even though these expenses are reimbursed, accounting for large expense reimbursements puts an extra burden on the bookkeeping staff and creates opportunities for mistakes or fraud.

PARKING SPACE

CONSIDER THIS

If you have your own parking lot or spaces designated for your employees' use but not enough space for all employees, consider a policy such as this, which rotates the use of reserved spaces. In many organizations, reserved parking is viewed as the ultimate perk!

▶ CREATIVE APPROACH

(not common in small organizations)

▶ BY-THE-BOOK APPROACH

(see Leading-Edge policy)

▶ LEADING-EDGE APPROACH

Our facilities have limited access to parking, and we encourage you to take public transportation to work whenever possible.

Each month, one parking space at each of our facilities is designated for the Team Player of the Month. This designation is selected monthly by an anonymous vote of all regular staff at the facility. It goes to the one employee who gets the most votes that month for "teamwork above and beyond the call of duty."

Each year, our board of directors holds a luncheon honoring all employees selected as Team Players of the Month over the previous year.

CHAPTER TEN

Information and Communication

CONFIDENTIALITY OF VOICE MAIL AND ELECTRONIC MAIL

▶ CREATIVE APPROACH

Because our technological resources are limited, we ask you to refrain from using computers for personal business, including sending e-mail messages.

▶ BY-THE-BOOK APPROACH

By-the-Book employees use voice mail and electronic mail to communicate with others in the agency and to receive messages when these people are unavailable. Employees should be aware that voice mail and electronic mail messages are not private and are subject to review by the agency.

Time spent on-line on an agency-sponsored account should concern By-the-Book business only. Excessive personal use of an on-line e-mail account may result in a request for reimbursement or cancellation of access to the account or to e-mail.

▶ LEADING-EDGE APPROACH

Leading-Edge Agency recognizes that its employees have reasonable expectations of privacy with regard to the use of voice mail and e-mail, even when this use is restricted to agency business and the information is stored in agency computers.

Leading-Edge reserves the right to access and disclose the contents of employee voice mail and e-mail messages but will only do so when it has a legitimate business need and the urgency of the need is sufficiently strong to offset the organization's commitment to employee privacy.

Leading-Edge does not and will not monitor voice mail and e-mail messages as a routine matter. The agency may inspect the contents of voice mail and e-mail messages or information stored on computers in the course of an investigation or as necessary to locate substantive information that is not readily available by some other means. The agency may disclose a voice mail or e-mail message or information stored on computer to law enforcement officials if the organization has reason to do so.

Electronic "snooping" by any employee is a violation of agency policy and grounds for disciplinary action up to and including dismissal. We do not take the inspection of voice mail, e-mail, and computer records lightly, and any request for access to such information must be approved in advance by the executive director.

EMPLOYEE INFORMATION

▶ CREATIVE APPROACH

(see By-the-Book policy)

▶ BY-THE-BOOK APPROACH

It is important that personnel files contain up-to-date information regarding each employee. Employees should inform their supervisor immediately whenever there are changes in their personal data, such as address, telephone number, marital status, domestic partnership, number of dependents, and person to notify in case of emergency.

Employees have the right to inspect their personnel file during regular office hours, given reasonable notice to the agency. An appointment to inspect the file may be made with the director of operations, who will accompany the employee while he or she inspects the file. Employees may obtain copies of any document in their personnel file to the extent required by law. Personnel records are the property of By-the-Book Agency and are not allowed to leave the office of the director of operations without authorization.

No reference information other than a verification of dates of employment, wages, and job titles will be given out to a third party without prior written authorization by the employee.

▶ LEADING-EDGE APPROACH

Your individual personnel file is kept in the human resources department. If you want to review its contents, you may make an appointment to do so at any time during normal operating hours. A member of the human resources staff must be present when you review your file, and files may not be removed from the department. You may, however, obtain copies of any document in your file.

Your personnel file is treated as confidential by Leading-Edge Agency. The information it contains is available to you, your manager, the human resources staff, the executive director, and others

CONSIDER THIS

For many employees, personnel files loom large in the imagination as repositories of huge amounts of secret (and perhaps negative) information. The best way to combat this fantasy is to have a clear policy telling employees that they can review their files at any time, with advance notice—it is their legal right.

It's a good idea for employers to limit the contents of personnel files to documents that employees have seen and, preferably, signed. In the rare instance when the contents of a file are subpoenaed, they will not yield any surprises.

as required by law or organizational necessity. Our policy with prospective employers is to verify an employee's position, dates of employment, and salary only.

We will not, under any circumstances, give out your home phone number or address.

AGENCY CONFIDENTIALITY

▶ CREATIVE APPROACH

Confidential information obtained during or through employment with Creative Agency may not be used by any staff member for the purpose of furthering current or future outside employment or activities or for obtaining personal gain or profit.

At no time should a staff member disclose nonpublic or sensitive information to individuals other than on a need-to-know basis.

▶ BY-THE-BOOK APPROACH

(see Creative Approach policy)

▶ LEADING-EDGE APPROACH

All records, history, and discussions about the people we serve must be considered private and kept in confidence. The very fact that an individual is served by Leading-Edge Agency can be disclosed only under specified conditions, which are described below, for reasons relating to law enforcement and fulfillment of our mission.

Employees may not disclose any information about a person, including the fact that the person is or is not served by our organization, to anyone outside this organization unless so permitted by the executive director or other authorized personnel. The principle of confidentiality must be maintained in all programs, departments, functions, and activities.

Information about clients of Leading-Edge Agency can be disclosed only under the following circumstances:

- If a release-of-information form is explained to and completed by the person the information is about before it is released.
- If records are inspected by an outside agency. The individuals who inspect records must be specifically authorized to do so by the executive director. The taking of notes and copying or removal of records are specifically prohibited in such cases.
- If we are required to do so by law.

CONSIDER THIS

It's particularly important for social service organizations working directly with clients to establish a confidentiality policy.

If your organization works with sensitive or proprietary information on a regular basis, you may want to have employees sign a confidentiality agreement, in addition to having a confidentiality policy.

Employees are specifically instructed not to release to state, federal, or other agencies information about any individuals or their records that would enable any person served to be identified by name, address, Social Security number, or other coding procedures, unless the employee is authorized to do so by the executive director.

Failure to follow these client confidentiality procedures will be grounds for immediate dismissal.

SPEAKING TO THE MEDIA

▶ CREATIVE APPROACH

(see policies for the other approaches)

▶ BY-THE-BOOK APPROACH

By-the-Book Agency has designated the director of communications as the person responsible for speaking with the press and making written and oral statements for publication. Any request for information or interviews by the media should be referred to the director of communications or the executive director.

▶ LEADING-EDGE APPROACH

It is our goal to give the press clear, consistent, and up-to-date information about our organization and its programs and services. Because information about our activities changes often, it is especially important not to give the press information that is inaccurate or misleading. Please refer all calls from reporters for the media (newspapers, magazines, radio, television, news agencies, other news services) to our vice president for public affairs or to the executive director.

CONSIDER THIS

A media relations policy is particularly useful in times of trouble—for instance, in the event of budget cuts or changes in senior management. It also helps ensure that you are putting out a consistent message about your programs and services.

INTERNAL COMMUNICATION

CONSIDER THIS

This type of policy provides you with an opportunity to encourage employees to take responsibility for keeping informed about general agency matters. It is helpful to point out to employees the various means by which you distribute information. An internal communication policy also allows you to spell out your right to determine what may be posted in the workplace.

▶ CREATIVE APPROACH

We use bulletin boards, mailboxes, and office e-mail to communicate important information to staff members on a regular basis. Each of our staff members is responsible for reading posted or distributed information on a timely basis.

▶ BY-THE-BOOK APPROACH

(see Creative Approach policy)

▶ LEADING-EDGE APPROACH

At Leading-Edge Agency, we believe that frequent, open communication of information about our operations, programs, and activities is an essential ingredient in maintaining a productive working environment. To encourage understanding and dialogue about our organization among all employees, we provide a number of formal vehicles to facilitate communication throughout the agency.

We publish a newsletter once a month. Employees who wish to contribute to the newsletter are encouraged to contact the human resources department. This department also publishes a weekly e-mail update, highlighting current activities and events. We maintain bulletin boards throughout our facilities for posting memos, job openings, and information about your rights as an employee. Last, we hold quarterly staff meetings to provide an opportunity for all employees to hear directly from members of our senior management team about our progress toward annual goals.

Leading-Edge Agency reserves the right to determine what may be posted on bulletin boards and to remove notices that are outdated or inappropriate for our work environment.

We expect you to read published and posted information and to attend meetings in order to keep informed about our activities and the opportunities that are available to you.

SOLICITATIONS

▶ CREATIVE APPROACH

No soliciting is allowed on agency premises. This includes requests for contributions to charitable organizations, as well as business advertising and the sale of goods (Girl Scout cookies, Tupperware, etc.).

▶ BY-THE-BOOK APPROACH

Solicitations and distributions are not permitted, except for annual charitable campaigns (such as United Way) that are formally approved by the board of directors. Activities that are not permitted include the following:

- Solicitation by an employee during work time
- Solicitation by an employee not on work time of an employee who is on work time
- Any solicitation or distribution by nonemployees
- Distribution of advertising materials or literature of any kind in work areas

  For the purposes of this policy, the following definitions apply:

- *Solicitation* includes, but is not limited to, any request for signatures, contributions, support of political activities, merchandise purchases, and organizing activities.
- *Distribution* includes, but is not limited to, passing out of literature, pamphlets, leaflets, or notices of any kind.
- *Work time* means all hours an employee is or should be working other than lunch or break time.
- *Work areas* are any area where agency work is regularly performed.

▶ LEADING-EDGE APPROACH

We do not permit solicitation, money collection, or the sale of merchandise by one employee to another while either employee is on work time. Work time is all time spent on our premises, in travel

CONSIDER THIS

We are all subjected to solicitation on the streets and in our homes (via the mail and phones)—we don't need to feel pressured to listen to someone else's sales pitch at work. If you have such a policy, it is important to enforce it consistently. If you can't sell Tupperware at work, then you also can't sell your grandchild's Girl Scout cookies.

While you do want to maintain a productive and work-focused environment, you don't want to stifle employees. One way to allow for some "free speech" is to designate one bulletin board on which employees can post—with prior approval—notices about cars for sale, cookie and bake sales, raffle tickets, theater performances, lectures, and other non-work-related events of potential interest to employees.

to or from one of our facilities, or on agency business, other than meal periods and break times.

We likewise prohibit the distribution of literature and the circulation of petitions or advertisements at any time. Finally, soliciting or distributing any literature by a nonemployee is prohibited on all agency property.

CHAPTER ELEVEN

Standards of Conduct

HARASSMENT

▶ CREATIVE APPROACH

It is illegal to harass others on the basis of their sex, sexual orientation, age, race, color, national origin, religion, marital or veteran status, citizenship, disability, or other personal characteristics. Harassment includes making derogatory remarks about such characteristics, making jokes about ethnic or other groups, and other verbal, physical, and visual behavior.

Sexual harassment is also prohibited. Propositions, repeated requests for dates, dirty jokes, sexually provocative pictures or cartoons, and other verbal, physical, and visual harassment of a sexual nature are prohibited. The harassment of any staff member will lead to immediate disciplinary action up to and including termination.

Any staff member who feels harassed has the right to file a charge with the Equal Employment Opportunity Commission and with a state agency. Before doing so, we ask that you first speak with your manager. If your manager is not an appropriate person, speak with our executive director or a member of the board's Personnel Committee, so that appropriate internal action may be taken. It is the responsibility of all managers to listen to such complaints and to refer them to the appropriate authority. We will not retaliate against any staff member who makes a claim of harassment.

▶ BY-THE-BOOK APPROACH

It is the policy of the agency that there shall be no harassment of any employee by fellow employees or by any supervisor on account of an employee's sex, race, national origin, religion, physical handicap, or sexual orientation (or on account of any other protected status).

The agency does not condone and will not permit such harassment of any employee and, in particular, will not tolerate the making of unwelcome sexual advances to any employee, unwelcome physical, verbal, or visual behavior that is sexual in nature, or the making of remarks or jokes known to be offensive to any

CONSIDER THIS

Due to a U.S. Supreme Court ruling in November 1993, employers are now responsible for ensuring that the workplace is free of factors that can create a "hostile working environment," in which a reasonable person would find it difficult to do his or her work. Do not tolerate sexual joking, innuendos, or sexually offensive comments or visual materials in your offices or work facilities.

It is important to state that all complaints will be promptly investigated and that no retaliation will be taken against any employee who files a complaint in good faith.

It is not enough to simply have a policy against harassment—you should provide information about this policy at the orientation session and should also provide some sort of consistent education or training for all your employees about what constitutes harassment and how to prevent it in your workplace.

employee because of his or her sex, age, race, national origin, re-ligion, physical handicap, or sexual orientation. An employee who believes that he or she has been treated in violation of this policy should immediately report the matter to the chair of the Person-nel Committee. The Personnel Committee will seek to investigate all complaints or violations of this policy promptly in as discreet a manner as possible.

▶ LEADING-EDGE APPROACH

(see policies for the other approaches)

WORKPLACE CONDUCT

▶ CREATIVE APPROACH

We have developed certain guidelines to reflect what we believe are good business practices. We strive to develop and maintain a pleasant, efficient, and fair work environment that fosters cooperation and understanding.

All staff members are expected to be:

- On time and ready for work at the beginning of their workday
- Careful and conscientious in the performance of their work
- Respectful and considerate of others
- Courteous and helpful when dealing with other staff members and with volunteers, supporters, and the general public

▶ BY-THE-BOOK APPROACH

Every organization has certain guidelines that are developed to reflect sound operational practices. This agency requires of its employees discipline, cooperation, efficiency, and productivity. It has set out standards of behavior with which all employees are required to comply. Failure to comply with these standards will result in disciplinary action, up to and including termination. Examples of conduct that may require disciplinary action include, but are not limited to, any of the following:

- Substandard job performance
- Failure to carry out job responsibilities
- Being absent from work without prior notification to supervisor
- Any safety violation
- Excessive tardiness or absenteeism
- Unauthorized overtime
- Rudeness or discourtesy toward a fellow employee, supervisor, volunteer, supporter, or member of the general public

CONSIDER THIS

The primary purpose of any employee handbook is to establish clear expectations: both of what you expect from an employee and of what an employee can expect from your organization as a place of employment. A "Workplace Conduct" section is the place where you can put across your basic expectations of professional behavior and the ways in which your organization will deal with performance and conduct problems. Take advantage of this opportunity to articulate your standards and your organization's disciplinary philosophy.

▶ LEADING-EDGE APPROACH

All employees at Leading-Edge Agency share responsibility for observing certain standards of conduct. These standards emphasize personal and professional integrity in all activities. Generally, treating others with the respect and consideration with which you expect to be treated and maintaining open, ongoing communication with your manager and coworkers will create a basis for a successful work experience.

It is the obligation and responsibility of each employee at Leading-Edge Agency to work on resolving problems and conflicts by focusing on solutions, keeping issues work-related (as opposed to personal), and communicating directly with the person or persons with whom you have a conflict. In most cases, discussing a situation will clear it up.

OPEN-DOOR POLICY

▶ CREATIVE APPROACH

All staff members are encouraged to provide input and suggestions concerning the overall operations and programs of Creative Agency, following appropriate communication channels. Staff members should initially bring their comments to their own manager. If that is for any reason inappropriate, staff members may speak directly with the executive director.

We operate in an open-door manner. All input from staff will be considered and can be presented without fear of personal recrimination.

▶ BY-THE-BOOK APPROACH

(see Leading-Edge Approach)

▶ LEADING-EDGE APPROACH

Leading-Edge Agency has an open-door policy that encourages employee participation in decisions that will affect them and their daily professional responsibilities. This policy also encourages employees who have job-related problems or complaints to talk them over with their supervisor or a manager at any level of management who they feel can help them. Leading-Edge believes that employee concerns are best addressed through informal and open communication.

The agency will attempt to keep all such expressions of concern, their investigation, and the terms of their resolution confidential. However, in the course of investigating and resolving concerns, some dissemination of information to others may be appropriate.

No employee will be disciplined or otherwise penalized for raising a concern in good faith.

CONSIDER THIS

Most organizations operate with an informal open-door policy, meaning that employees are encouraged to speak frankly to their supervisor or other appropriate members of management about job-related concerns.

DISCIPLINARY PROCEDURES

CONSIDER THIS

Regardless of the specifics of your organization's approach to discipline, you should have a disciplinary process that is generally progressive. Just as important, you should state that some problems will result in immediate termination and that it is at management's discretion to decide what step in a disciplinary process is most appropriate. (See also Involuntary Termination in Chapter Twelve.)

▶ CREATIVE APPROACH

DISCIPLINARY ACTION

The primary objective of any disciplinary action is to improve job performance. Actions by a staff member that are inappropriate for the work environment, are a hindrance to effective job performance, or violate agency policy constitute improper conduct and may be cause for disciplinary action.

Creative Agency maintains a progressive and participatory disciplinary system, which may include some or all of the following steps:

1. Documented oral warning
2. Written warning
3. Final written warning
4. Dismissal

Based on circumstances, a manager may choose to enter into disciplinary action at any step in the process, including immediate dismissal. All disciplinary action beyond oral warning requires the approval of the executive director.

▶ BY-THE-BOOK APPROACH

CORRECTIVE ACTION

The corrective action process is designed to protect the safety and promote the fair treatment of all employees. Discipline may be required for substandard job performance, safety violations, absenteeism, or inability to work as part of a team. By-the-Book supervisors are responsible for identifying problems and assisting in their resolution. Any discipline involving suspension or discharge must be reviewed and approved by the executive director.

There are four levels of corrective action, any one of which may be entered into, depending on the circumstances and severity of the problem:

1. *Employee Counseling or Verbal Warning.* The supervisor counsels the employee following a minor offense in an effort to eliminate possible misunderstandings and to identify what constitutes good performance. The supervisor will help the employee develop a solution and improve performance to the appropriate level. Verbal warnings are documented by the supervisor and signed by the employee.

2. *Written Warning.* The employee meets with his or her supervisor and is presented with a written notice of corrective action. A written warning is designed to make sure that the employee is fully aware of the misconduct or performance problem, including the degree of seriousness and the consequences if the problem is not corrected. The supervisor and employee set a time frame during which improvement must be made and maintained, and a check-in process is determined. Employees on written warning are not eligible for promotions, transfers, or pay increases unless specifically approved by the executive director.

3. *Suspension.* Employees who are suspected of serious misconduct may be suspended with pay in situations where an investigation is required prior to final action being taken.

4. *Discharge.* In cases of serious misconduct, immediate rather than progressive corrective action may be taken. Termination can result from a single serious offense, or it can be the final step in a process to correct a series of minor offenses of the same nature. It can also occur as the result of ongoing conduct that is inconsistent with agency policy.

An employee may be suspended with pay pending an investigation of a charge of serious misconduct.

▶ LEADING-EDGE APPROACH

PERFORMANCE IMPROVEMENT

It may become necessary for you and your manager to address a problem by identifying unacceptable behavior and establishing a clear plan for correcting it. This usually occurs after informal attempts to resolve the situation have failed.

This process, called performance improvement, is a progressive process that includes the following steps:

1. A formal performance counseling session with your manager
2. A written performance improvement plan
3. Termination of employment or completion of performance improvement plan

This process is designed to facilitate clear, precise, and timely communication about problems and the development of solutions.

Employees who are in the performance improvement process are not eligible for raises, promotions, or transfers until the process has been satisfactorily completed. Although performance improvement is usually a progressive process, managers may choose to move to any step in the process, including immediate termination of employment, based on the severity of the problem or misconduct and the circumstances.

Some examples of conduct that may require beginning the formal performance improvement process are as follows:

- Substandard job performance
- Failure to carry out job responsibilities
- Inability to work effectively with others
- Excessive absenteeism or tardiness
- Unauthorized overtime

Managers are required to enlist the support of the human resources department when entering into the performance improvement process. Termination of employment requires the review and approval of the executive director.

COMPLAINT PROCEDURES

▶ CREATIVE APPROACH

EMPLOYEE APPEAL PROCESS

As a matter of general policy, managers at all levels will provide an open door for discussion and a receptive ear and will review all staff member suggestions or complaints concerning our work practices and procedures.

If a staff member wishes to make a formal complaint, it should be done within a reasonable time after the incident has occurred or the issue has arisen. We consider an open discussion between employee and manager as the first step in the complaint procedure. The manager must respond to the complaint in a timely manner. If the manager does not resolve the complaint within a reasonable time frame or if the staff member disagrees with the manager's solution, the staff member may appeal directly to the executive director.

At this point, the complaint must be written down, with the nature of the grievance clearly outlined. The executive director will investigate the complaint and notify the staff member, in writing, of a decision within a reasonable amount of time.

As a last resort, a staff member may take a complaint to the Personnel Committee of the board of directors. The Personnel Committee's decision constitutes the agency's final word on the matter.

▶ BY-THE-BOOK APPROACH

GRIEVANCE PROCEDURE

Any employee who has a complaint concerning an agency policy or its application has the right to file a grievance according to procedures outlined in this policy. No employee will be discriminated against, harassed, or intimidated or will suffer any reprisal as a result of filing a grievance or participating in the investigation of a grievance. If an employee feels that he or she is being subjected to any reprisal, that employee has the right to appeal directly to the executive director.

> **CONSIDER THIS**
>
> A complaint procedure, when clearly spelled out and adhered to, allows employees to voice concerns in a constructive manner and contributes to a sense of fairness and balance in the workplace. Complaint procedures will be scrutinized by the employees who use them, so do not commit to a process (time frames, for instance) unless you are prepared to follow it consistently.

Employees should attempt to resolve the problem informally with their supervisor as soon as possible. If a solution cannot be reached, the employee may present a formal grievance, in writing, to the executive director.

All complaints will be handled in a timely manner. By-the-Book Agency's goal is to resolve a complaint within twenty (20) working days from the time of its initiation. If an extension or a reduction of the time limit becomes necessary, all parties involved will be notified. Employees may not file grievance procedures challenging the substance of a performance evaluation.

▶ LEADING-EDGE APPROACH

INTERNAL COMPLAINT REVIEW

The purpose of the internal complaint review is to provide all employees of Leading-Edge Agency with the opportunity to seek internal resolution of work-related complaints. This policy supplements the open-door policy set forth in this handbook, which states our philosophy that all employees have free access to their immediate supervisors or to other supervisors of their choice to express their work-related concerns informally.

We will attempt to treat all internal complaints and their investigation as confidential, recognizing, however, that in the course of investigating and resolving internal complaints, some dissemination of information to others may be appropriate.

PROCEDURE

Written complaints should be directed to the executive director as soon as possible after the date of the event that gave rise to the work-related concern, but no later than ten (10) days following such event.

The executive director (or an authorized designee) will set up a meeting to discuss the complaint within a reasonable time following the receipt of the written complaint. As necessary, the executive director (or designee) will also meet with others who are named in the complaint or who may have knowledge of the facts set forth in the complaint.

Within ten (10) working days of the last of these meetings, the executive director will provide the employee with a written response to the complaint. (This time frame may be changed according to circumstances.) If the complaint is resolved to the employee's satisfaction, the terms of the resolution will be recorded and signed by the employee and the executive director.

APPEAL

If the complaint is related to the termination of an employee and if the employee is not satisfied with the decision of the executive director, the employee may take the matter to arbitration, but only if the employee agrees in writing that the arbitration decision will be final and may not be relitigated in court. If the employee agrees to arbitration as the final solution, Leading-Edge Agency will pay the arbitrator's fee. Arbitrators will be selected in accordance with the rules of the American Arbitration Association. Inclusion of this arbitration provision is not intended to alter the at-will status of anyone's employment.

NONRETALIATION

No employee who has filed a complaint in good faith will be unlawfully disciplined or otherwise retaliated against, even if Leading-Edge Agency does not agree with the complaint.

CONFLICT OF INTEREST

▶ CREATIVE APPROACH

We are proud of our reputation for conducting our activities with fairness and integrity. We require all our staff members to uphold this reputation in every work-related activity. Be particularly careful to avoid situations where personal gain may influence a work-related situation or relationships that might influence or affect your judgment on the job. If you are ever in doubt about whether an activity meets our high ethical standards or compromises our reputation, please discuss your concerns with your manager or our executive director.

▶ BY-THE-BOOK APPROACH

It is important that employees avoid conflicts of interest to maintain high standards of conduct. A conflict of interest is a situation in which an employee's private or economic interest interferes with or in any way influences the employee's duties and responsibilities at By-the-Book Agency or with the agency's general activities, even if this conflict has no adverse impact on job performance.

Employees must advise the executive director of any outside employment (on either a salary or a fee basis). Any employee needing advice about a potential conflict of interest should consult with the director of operations or the executive director. If an employee's outside activity is determined to constitute a conflict of interest and the activity continues beyond a reasonable amount of time, disciplinary action will result, up to and including termination of employment.

▶ LEADING-EDGE APPROACH

We expect all our employees to use good judgment, to adhere to high ethical standards, and to avoid situations that create an actual or potential conflict of interest between the employee's interests and the interests of Leading-Edge Agency. If you are unsure as to whether a certain transaction, activity, or relationship, including outside employment, constitutes a conflict of interest, you should discuss it with our director of human resources or the director of operations. Our executive director must approve any exceptions to this guideline in writing.

We intend that this conflict-of-interest policy be interpreted fairly so that we do not create harsh results when a conflict arises. If an employee violates this policy through no fault of his or her own or unintentionally, the employee will be given a reasonable amount of time (as determined by the executive director) to comply with our policy.

Nevertheless, you should know that failure to adhere to these guidelines, including failure to disclose any conflicts or to seek an exception, may result in discipline, up to and including termination of employment.

FRATERNIZATION

CONSIDER THIS

Fraternization policies are a necessity for organizations providing direct service to individuals in the community. Some nonprofit social service organizations hire and train individuals they formerly served, in which case a fraternization policy becomes even more essential. Make sure your employees understand that inappropriate relationships can undermine your programs or create the appearance of favoritism, and then make sure they know you will strictly enforce your fraternization policy.

▶ ALL APPROACHES

The agency strictly prohibits employees from fraternizing with any of the people served by our programs. Fraternizing is defined as pursuing a close friendship or intimate relationship with a current client. We also prohibit the transfer of money or goods between employees and persons currently or formerly served.

If evidence of nonprofessional, non-work-related interaction between an employee and any person served by this agency is found, we will conduct a thorough investigation to determine if there has been a violation of our fraternization policy. If a policy violation is proven, the employee will be dismissed, and a report will be filed with the appropriate authorities if vulnerable adults are involved.

Employees are further required to exercise good judgment in establishing nonprofessional, non-work-related relationships with persons formerly served by our programs. In general, we discourage such relationships at any time. If you have a concern about a potential personal relationship with a former client, please discuss it in confidence with our director of human resources.

FEES AND HONORARIA

▶ CREATIVE APPROACH

(not common in small organizations)

▶ BY-THE-BOOK APPROACH

When staff members consult, lecture, counsel, or advise outside individuals or organizations on behalf of By-the-Book Agency, all fees, donations, or cash honoraria must be paid to the agency.

▶ LEADING-EDGE APPROACH

(see By-the-Book Approach)

CONSIDER THIS

An employee who speaks, consults, or lectures as part of the job generally assumes that his or her salary is compensation for such activities. But if additional fees or honoraria are paid for these employee activities, it is wise to set out a simple policy determining who gets to keep these funds.

RELATIONS WITH SUPPLIERS

CONSIDER THIS

Depending on the frequency with which your organization does business with outside vendors and contractors, you may choose to include this policy or feel it isn't needed. Setting clear limits on gifts from suppliers can prevent problems from developing over time. Without having read such a policy, some employees may not even consider the possibility that they appear to be engaging in favoritism or inappropriate supplier relations.

▶ CREATIVE APPROACH

(not common in small organizations)

▶ BY-THE-BOOK APPROACH

From time to time, employees may be offered gifts, entertainment, or other favors from a supplier, contractor, or organization with which By-the-Book has business dealings. No employee of By-the-Book Agency may accept any item of value aside from nominal gifts and common courtesies.

Furthermore, all employees should understand that entering into a personal relationship with a subordinate employee or with an employee of a supplier, contractor, or other organization having financial dealings with By-the-Book Agency creates a possible conflict of interest that requires full disclosure to the agency.

▶ LEADING-EDGE APPROACH

While Leading-Edge Agency encourages you to have friendly relations with suppliers and contractors, you must always base your business decisions solely on our organization's needs and the quality of the product or service supplied.

Generally, you should not accept gifts, favors, entertainment, free services, discounts on personal purchases, or any other special considerations for yourself or your family that are not offered to all other agency employees. Gifts received from suppliers during the holidays should be shared with our entire staff.

All your dealings should be conducted in an open, honest, professional, and completely ethical manner. If you have any questions about what may be perceived as ethical or unethical, please talk with your manager.

PART FIVE

Clarifying End-of-Employment Policies

CHAPTER TWELVE

Ending Employment

AT-WILL STATUS

▶ CREATIVE APPROACH

We hope to retain good employees. However, employment at Creative Agency is for no specified time, regardless of length of service. Just as you are free to leave at any time, for any reason, we reserve the same right to end our employment relationship with you at any time, with or without notice, for any reason not prohibited by law.

No policy contained in this handbook should be interpreted as in any way changing your at-will status.

▶ BY-THE-BOOK APPROACH

Employment with By-the-Book Agency is not for any specified period and can be terminated by either the employee or the agency at any time with or without any particular reason or advance notice. Nothing contained in these policies is intended to, or should be construed to, alter the at-will relationship between By-the-Book Agency and its employees. Although other terms and conditions and benefits of employment with By-the-Book may change from time to time, the at-will relationship of employment is one aspect that cannot be changed except by an agreement in writing with the board of directors, signed by the chair of the board on behalf of the entire board.

▶ LEADING-EDGE APPROACH

At Leading-Edge Agency, we are committed to the philosophy that employment relationships are both personal and voluntary. By this we mean that although we hope for mutually beneficial working relationships with our employees, we recognize that changing circumstances make it impossible to guarantee employment. Your employment with Leading-Edge Agency has no specified duration, and either you or the agency may end the employment relationship whenever either of us believes it is best to do so, without consideration of cause or notice.

CONSIDER THIS

Many states allow "at-will employment." This is an employment, having no specified term, that may be terminated at the will of either party on notice to the other. Employment for a specified term means an employment for a period greater than one month.

There are two compelling reasons to institute an at-will policy for your organization. First, it provides you with a strong defense against unlawful termination lawsuits. Second, it allows you the latitude to dismiss employees for inappropriate behavior or substandard job performance, or to eliminate jobs out of economic necessity.

While we maintain and revise written and other personnel policies in order to adapt to changing organizational needs, any personnel policies or programs that may be in effect from time to time do not affect our policy of voluntary employment relationships. The voluntary nature of our employment relationship may not be changed except by a separate written agreement specifically entered into for such purpose and signed by our board president.

VOLUNTARY TERMINATION OF EMPLOYMENT

▶ CREATIVE APPROACH

Any staff member may voluntarily resign at any time and for any reason. We will also consider that you have resigned if you do not return from an approved leave of absence on the specified return date or fail to report to work without notice for three (3) consecutive days.

We ask you to give a minimum of two (2) weeks' written notice of resignation if at all possible.

▶ BY-THE-BOOK APPROACH

Any employee may voluntarily resign at any time and for any reason. Employees will be considered to have resigned if either of the following events occurs:

- Failure to return from an approved leave of absence on the specified return date
- Failure to report to work without notice for three (3) consecutive days

All employees are asked to give a minimum of two (2) weeks' written notice of resignation. If an employee is asked to leave our employ before the end of the notice period (for example, if a replacement is to begin immediately), the employee will be paid for the entire notice period.

Employees are required to turn over all keys and other agency property to the office manager before leaving on their last day of work.

▶ LEADING-EDGE APPROACH

If you decide to resign from your job at Leading-Edge Agency, we ask that you give a minimum of two (2) weeks' notice. Please submit a letter of resignation to your manager.

CONSIDER THIS

Although employees are free to leave their jobs with no notice, it is effective to spell out your request that they give two (2) weeks' notice. It is also wise to spell out a job abandonment policy so as to avoid misunderstandings if an employee disappears and then reappears expecting to continue working.

You are considered to have resigned if you do not return from a leave of absence, turn down a comparable position offered upon return from a leave of absence, or have an unexcused or unreported absence of two (2) consecutive days.

Before leaving on your last day of work, you must return all agency property, including keys, credit cards, computer equipment, and all documents issued to you during the course of your employment.

INVOLUNTARY TERMINATION

▶ ALL APPROACHES

This agency reserves the right to terminate any employee at any time, with or without cause or notice. Generally, when an employee is believed, in the opinion of his or her supervisor, to have a job performance problem or to be engaging in behavior that is unacceptable or counterproductive, the employee will be given an opportunity to improve his or her performance or behavior to an acceptable level by means of a formal disciplinary action process. However, the following list, though not complete, gives examples of behavior that can result in immediate termination of employment:

- Breaching confidentiality
- Violating the drug- and alcohol-free workplace policy
- Theft—including, but not limited to, the removal of agency property or the property of another employee from agency premises without prior authorization
- Walking off the job without supervisory approval
- Working for another employer while on a leave of absence without the prior consent of this agency
- Fighting, roughhousing, abusive language, or conduct that is hostile or disrespectful toward a coworker, supervisor, board member, volunteer, or any person associated with or served by this agency
- Disregarding established safety procedures; knowingly creating an unsafe work situation for self or any coworker
- Falsifying or altering records or time sheets
- Refusing to perform a work-related duty when directly instructed to do so by a supervisor or member of management
- Possessing a weapon or firearm on this agency's property
- Unauthorized use or dissemination of proprietary information
- Violating this agency's equal opportunity or harassment policies
- Unauthorized use of agency property, including vehicles

All involuntary terminations require review by the executive director.

CONSIDER THIS

By listing numerous examples of unacceptable behavior that can be grounds for dismissal, you are providing clear guidelines for standards of behavior. Employees need to understand, in no uncertain terms, the actions and behaviors that will not be tolerated in your workplace. It is equally important that you clearly state that these are examples of unacceptable behavior and not an exhaustive or complete list.

JOB ELIMINATION AND LAYOFFS

CONSIDER THIS

Given the financial challenges of running a nonprofit, it is wise to include a layoff policy in your handbook. The larger and more structured your organization is, the more detailed and specific your policy should be. In general, employees are most concerned with notice, the decision-making process, and severance pay policies.

► CREATIVE APPROACH

From time to time, we may need to lay off an employee as a result of reorganization, job elimination, funding changes, or lack of work. Should such a termination be necessary, all affected staff members will be given as much advance notice as possible.

If you lose your job due to a layoff or reorganization, you will receive all accrued, unused vacation pay, plus one (1) week of severance pay for each year of employment up to a maximum of eight (8) weeks' pay. You also will be eligible for continuation of your benefits coverage, based on the specifics of COBRA (see the health insurance continuation policies in Part Three for more information).

► BY-THE-BOOK APPROACH

If it becomes necessary to reduce or change the composition of the agency's workforce, the executive director, in consultation with the Personnel Committee of the board of directors, will decide which jobs will be eliminated.

Regular full- and part-time employees who have worked at least one (1) calendar year and whose positions are eliminated by a workforce reduction may receive a severance allowance. Generally, severance pay is equal to one (1) week of pay for every full year of employment, to a maximum of twelve (12) weeks' pay. The executive director, with approval of the board, at the time of a workforce reduction will set the agency's exact severance policy.

► LEADING-EDGE APPROACH

Given the realities of the nonprofit sector, cutbacks or job reductions may be unavoidable due to changes in programs, funding, or forces beyond our control. Leading-Edge Agency will strive to minimize the negative impact on current employees if a reduction in the workforce becomes necessary.

In the case where a program may have to be reduced in size or eliminated entirely, Leading-Edge will reduce staff progressively, using the following steps:

1. Voluntary reductions in staff size. This includes employees who agree to early retirement, a leave of absence, or a reduction in hours.

2. Attrition.

3. Possible elimination of part-time positions before full-time positions.

4. Transfer of employees to other vacant positions within our operations, provided they meet the minimum qualifications of the positions.

When determining which regular employees are laid off, our executive director may implement a seniority system giving consideration to such factors as the following, among others:

- Performance evaluations
- Length of service
- Job specialty, responsibilities, and special skills
- Supervisory input

All affected employees will receive notice of a layoff in writing from the executive director at least thirty (30) days prior to the layoff date. Employees who receive shorter notice will receive pay in lieu of notice for the difference between receipt of actual notice and thirty (30) days.

Laid-off employees will be paid for any accrued, unused vacation time. Employees will also receive one (1) week of severance pay for every full year of service. Laid-off employees currently enrolled in Leading-Edge Agency's health insurance program will be offered the opportunity to continue the same coverage for up to eighteen (18) months by paying the cost of the monthly premium.

EXIT INTERVIEWS

▶ CREATIVE APPROACH

To the greatest extent possible, exit interviews will be conducted with all staff members who leave our employ.

▶ BY-THE-BOOK APPROACH

The executive director will conduct a confidential interview with each employee who voluntarily terminates employment with By-the-Book prior to the last day of work. These conversations enable the agency to gather important information about personnel policies and procedures that may be of benefit to many other employees. Although exit interviews are not mandatory, employees are encouraged to participate in them and to speak frankly about their employment experience with By-the-Book Agency.

▶ LEADING-EDGE APPROACH

A member of our human resources staff meets with all regular employees on or before their last day of work. This exit interview is meant to provide employees with the opportunity to reflect on their experience at Leading-Edge Agency and to offer comments, advice, or suggestions pertaining to our work policies and practices.

Information shared during an exit interview will be treated as confidential and acted on in an appropriate and timely manner.

Resources

A. List of Legally Required Policies

The following legally required policies are found in the chapters indicated below.

B. State-by-State Provisions for Selected Policies

AMERICANS WITH DISABILITIES ACT

These sources can provide additional information about the ADA.

INFORMATION ABOUT EMPLOYMENT PROVISIONS

Equal Employment Opportunity Commission
1801 L Street, N.W.
Washington, DC 20507
(202) 663-4900

INFORMATION ABOUT PUBLIC ACCOMMODATION PROVISIONS

Office of the ADA
Civil Rights Division
U.S. Department of Justice
P.O. Box 66738
Washington, DC 20035
(800) 514-0301

Architectural and Transportation Barriers Compliance Board
1331 F Street, N.W., Suite 1000
Washington, DC 20004-1111
(800) 872-2253

EQUAL EMPLOYMENT OPPORTUNITY

Check with your state's labor department or attorney general's office to direct you to the proper enforcement agency.

ALABAMA

No true antidiscrimination law, but you're encouraged to employ people who are blind or otherwise physically disabled (Ala. Code §21-71-1). If you have an affirmative action program, the term *minority,* in addition to an ethnic group or other classification, includes American Indians or Alaskan Natives, as identified by birth certificates or tribal records (Ala. Code §25-1-10). *Enforcing agency:* None

ALASKA

Race, religion, color, national origin, age, physical disability, gender, marital status, or changes in marital status: Alaska Human Rights Law (Alaska Stat. §18.80.110). Pregnancy or parenthood (Alaska Stat. §18.80.220). Mental illness. (Alaska Stat. §47.30.865). *Enforcing agency:* Human Rights Commission, 800 A Street, Suite 204, Anchorage, AK 99501; (907) 274-4692.

ARIZONA

Race, color, religion, gender, age, physical disability (excluding current alcohol or drug use), AIDS, and national origin: Arizona Civil Rights Act (Ariz. Rev. Stat. Ann. §41-1401). *Enforcing agency:* Civil Rights Division, 1275 West Washington Street, Phoenix, AZ 85007; (602) 542-5263.

ARKANSAS

No general discrimination law. Discrimination in wages on the basis of gender is prohibited (Ark. Code Ann. §11-4-601). *Enforcing agency:* None.

CALIFORNIA

Race, religious creed, religion, color, national origin, ancestry, physical disability, mental disability, medical condition, marital status, gender, age (if forty years old or older), pregnancy, childbirth, or related medical conditions (Calif. Govt. Code §§12940, 12941, 12945). AIDS or HIV: if an employee's participation in a research study regarding AIDS or HIV is disclosed, you can't use that information to determine the employability or insurability of that person (Calif. Health & Safety Code §121115). Political activities or affiliations, including sexual orientation (Calif. Lab. Code §§1101, 1102, and 1102.1). *Enforcing agency:* Department of Fair Employment and Housing, 2014 T Street, Suite 210, Sacramento, CA 95814; (916) 445-9918.

COLORADO

Race, religion color, age, gender, national origin, ancestry: Fair Employment Practices Act (Colo. Rev. Stat. §24-34-401). Physical or mental disability (Colo. Rev. Stat. §27-10-115). *Enforcing agency:* Civil Rights Commission, 1560 Broadway, Suite 1050, Denver, CO 80202-5143; (303) 894-2997.

CONNECTICUT

Race, color, religion, age, gender, pregnancy, marital status, sexual orientation, national origin, ancestry, present or previous mental or physical disability: Fair Employment Practices Act (Conn. Gen. Stat. Ann. §46a-60). *Enforcing agency:* Commission on Human Rights and Opportunities, 1229 Albany Avenue, Hartford, CT 06112; (203) 566-7710.

DELAWARE

Race, color, religion, gender, national origin, marital status, refusal to grant sexual favors, age (if between forty and seventy years old), or physical disability as long as the cost to you of accommodating the employee's physical disability doesn't exceed 5 percent of that employee's annual compensation: Fair Employment Practices Act (Del. Code Ann., t. 19, §710). *Enforcing agency:* Department of Labor, Labor Law Enforcement Section, State Office Building, 6th floor, 820 North French Street, Wilmington, DE 19801; (302) 577-2900.

DISTRICT OF COLUMBIA

Race, color, religion, national origin, age (if between the ages of eighteen and sixty-five), gender, personal appearance, marital status or family responsibilities, sexual orientation, political affiliation, matriculation, or physical disability: Human Rights Act (D.C. Code Ann. §1-2512). *Enforcing agency:* Human Rights Commission, 441 Fourth Street, N.W., Washington, DC 20001; (202) 724-1385.

FLORIDA

Race, color, religion, gender, national origin, age, marital status, physical disability, or political activity: Human Rights Act (Fla. Stat. Ann. §760-01). AIDS or HIV condition (Fla. Stat. Ann. §760-50). *Enforcing agency:* Commission on Human Relations, 325 John Knox Road, Building F, Suite 240, Tallahassee, FL 32303-4149; (904) 488-7082.

GEORGIA

Mental or physical disability (excluding the use of alcohol or any illegal or federally controlled drug) (Ga. Code Ann. §66-501). Age, if between forty and seventy years old (Ga. Code Ann. §§54-1102 and 54-9927). *Enforcing agency:* None.

HAWAII

Race, religion, color, ancestry, gender, sexual orientation, age, marital status, mental or physical disability, pregnancy, childbirth or related medical conditions: Fair Employment Practices Law (Hawaii Rev. Stat. §§378-1 et seq.). *Enforcing agency:* Hawaii Civil Rights Commission, 888 Mililani Street, 2nd floor, Honolulu, HI 96813; (808) 586-8640.

IDAHO

Race, color, religion, national origin, gender, age (if age forty or older), or physical or mental disability: Fair Employment Practices Act (Idaho Code §67-5901). *Enforcing agency:* Commission on Human Rights, 450 West State Street, Boise, ID 83720; (208) 334-2873.

ILLINOIS

Race, color, gender, national origin, ancestry, age, marital status, or physical or mental disability: Human Rights Act (Ill. Ann. Stat., ch. 68, §1-101). *Enforcing agency:* Department of Human Rights, James R. Thompson Center, 100 West Randolph Street, 10th floor, Chicago, IL 60601; (312) 814-6245.

INDIANA

Race, color, gender, national origin, ancestry, religion, age (if between forty and seventy years of age), or physical disability: Civil Rights Law (Ind. Code Ann. §22-9-1-1). *Enforcing agency:* Civil Rights Commission, 100 North Senate Avenue, Room N-103, Indianapolis, IN 46204; (317) 232-2600.

IOWA

Race, color, religion, age, gender, national origin, or physical disability: Civil Rights Act (Iowa Code Ann. §216.1). *Enforcing agency:* Civil Rights Commission, 211 East Maple Street, 2nd floor, Des Moines, IA 50319; (515) 281-4121.

KANSAS

Race, color, religion, gender, age (if over age eighteen), national origin or ancestry, or physical disability: Act Against Discrimination (Kans. Stat. Ann. §44-1001). *Enforcing agency:* Civil Rights Commission, Landon State Office Building, 900 S.W. Jackson Street, Suite 851 South, Topeka, KS 66612-1258; (913) 296-3206.

KENTUCKY

Race, color, religion, national origin, gender, or age (if between forty and seventy years of age): Civil Rights Act (Ky. Rev. Stat. §344-040). Physical disability (Ky. Rev. Stat. §207.130). *Enforcing agency:* Human Rights Commission, 332 West Broadway, 7th floor, Louisville, KY 40202; (502) 595-4024.

LOUISIANA

Race, color, religion, gender, national origin, pregnancy, or sickle-cell traits: Discrimination in Employment Act (La. Rev. Stat. Ann. §23:1001). Physical or mental disability (La. Rev. Stat. Ann. §46:2251). Age (if between forty and seventy years old) (La. Rev. Stat. Ann. §23:972). Participation in investigations relating to state's employment laws (La. Rev. Stat. Ann. §23.964). *Enforcing agency:* None.

MAINE

Race, color, gender, religion, national origin, ancestry, age, or physical or mental disability: Human Rights Act (Maine Rev. Stat. Ann., t. 5, §4572). *Enforcing agency:* Human Rights Commission, Statehouse, Station 51, Augusta, ME 04333; (207) 624-6050.

MARYLAND

Race, color, religion, gender, national origin, age, marital status, or past or current physical or mental illness or disability as long as the disability does not prevent the worker from performing the job: Human Relations Commission Act (Md. Code Ann., art. 49B, §16). *Enforcing agency:* Commission on Human Relations, 20 East Franklin Street, Baltimore, MD 21202; (301) 333-1700.

MASSACHUSETTS

Race, color, religion, gender, sexual orientation, national origin, ancestry, age, or physical or mental disability: Fair Employment Practices Act (Mass. Gen. Laws Ann., ch. 151B, §1). *Enforcing agency:* Commission Against Discrimination, One Ashburton Place, Boston, MA 02108; (617) 727-3990.

MICHIGAN

Race, color, religion, gender, national origin, height, weight, marital status, or age: Elliot Larsen Civil Rights Act (Mich. Stat. Ann. §§3.548(101) et seq.). Physical disability and mental disability (Mich. Stat. Ann. §§3.550(103) et seq.). *Enforcing agency:* Department of Civil Rights, 1200 6th Street, 7th floor, Detroit, MI 48226; (313) 256-2615.

MINNESOTA

Race, color, religion, creed, gender, marital status, sexual orientation, national origin, age, physical disability, or receipt of public assistance (Minn. Stat. Ann §363.03). *Enforcing agency:* Department of Human Rights, Bremer Tower, 7th Place and Minnesota Street, St. Paul, MN 55101; (612) 296-5663.

MISSISSIPPI

No statute for private employers.

MISSOURI

Race, color, religion, gender, national origin, ancestry, age (if between forty and seventy years old), or physical or mental disability: Human Rights Act (Mo. Ann. Stat. §213.055). AIDS condition, except individuals currently contagious and who pose a direct threat to the health and safety of others or who, because of current contagious disease, are unable to perform the duties of their employment (Mo. Ann. Stat. §191.655). *Enforcing agency:* Commission on Human Rights, 3315 West Truman Boulevard, Jefferson City, MO 65102-1129; (314) 751-3325.

MONTANA

Race, color, religion, creed, gender, age, national origin, marital status, or physical or mental disability: Human Rights Statute (Mont. Code Ann. §49-2-303). *Enforcing agency:* Human Rights Commission, 1236 Sixth Avenue, Helena, MT 59624; (406) 444-2884.

NEBRASKA

Race, color, religion, gender, national origin, age (between forty and seventy), marital status, or disability (excluding addiction to alcohol, other drugs, or gambling): Fair Employment Act (Nebr. Rev. Stat. Ann. §48-1104). *Enforcing agency:* Equal Opportunity Commission, 301 Centennial Mall South, Lincoln, NE 68509-4934; (402) 471-2024.

NEVADA

Race, color, religion, gender, age (if over forty years old), national origin, or physical disability: Fair Employment Practices Act (Nev. Rev. Stat. Ann. §613.330). *Enforcing agency:* Equal Rights Commission, 2450 Wrondel Way, Suite C, Reno, NV 89502; (702) 688-1288.

NEW HAMPSHIRE

Race, color, religion, gender, age, national origin, marital status, or physical or mental disability: Law Against Discrimination (N.H. Rev. Stat. Ann §354-A:1). *Enforcing agency:* Human Rights Commission, 163 Loudon Road, Concord, NH 03301; (603) 271-2767.

NEW JERSEY

Race, color, religion, gender, national origin, ancestry, age (if between forty and seventy years old), marital status, sexual or affectional orientation, atypical hereditary cellular or blood trait, past or present physical or mental disability, or draft liability for the armed forces: Law Against Discrimination (N.J. Stat. Ann. §10:5-12). *Enforcing agency:* Division of Civil Rights, 31 Clinton Street, 3rd floor, Newark, NJ 07102; (201) 648-2700.

NEW MEXICO

Race, color, religion, gender, age, national origin, ancestry, medical condition, or physical or mental disability: Human Rights Act (N.Mex. Stat. Ann. §28-1-7). *Enforcing agency:* Human Rights Commission, 1596 Pacheco Street, Aspen Plaza, Santa Fe, NM 87505; (505) 827-6838.

NEW YORK

Race, color, religion, creed, gender, age (if age eighteen or older), national origin, marital status, or physical or mental disability: Human Rights Law (N.Y. Exec. Law §296). *Enforcing agency:* Division of Human Rights, 55 West 125th Street, New York, NY 10027; (212) 961-8400.

NORTH CAROLINA

Race, color, religion, gender, age, national origin; applies only if you regularly employ more than fifteen employees: Equal Employment Practices Act (N.C. Gen. Stat. §143-422.2). Sickle-cell or hemoglobin C traits (N.C. Gen. Stat. §95-28.1). Physical or mental disability (N.C. Gen. Stat. §§168A-1 to A-5). AIDS or HIV condition; applies to discrimination against existing employees; statute specifically allows you to request applicants to take an AIDS test and to deny employment based solely on a positive test result (N.C. Gen. Stat. §130A-148). *Enforcing agency:* Human Relations Commission, 121 West Jones Street, Raleigh, NC 27603; (919) 733-7996.

NORTH DAKOTA

Race, color, religion, gender, national origin, age (if between forty and seventy years old), marital status, status with regard to public assistance, physical or mental disability, or participation in any lawful activity off your premises during nonworking hours (N.Dak. Cent. Code §14.02.4-03). *Enforcing agency:* None.

OHIO

Race, color, religion, gender, national origin, ancestry, age, or physical or mental disability: Civil Rights Act (Ohio Rev. Code Ann. §4112.02). Age (if forty years old or over) (Ohio Rev. Code Ann. §4107.17). *Enforcing agency:* Civil Rights Commission, 220 Parsons Avenue, Columbus, OH 43266-0543; (614) 466-5928.

OKLAHOMA

Race, color, religion, gender, national origin, age (if age forty or older), or physical disability; applies if you employ more than twenty people: Civil Rights Act (Okla. Stat. Ann., t. 25, §1302). *Enforcing agency:* Human Rights Commission, 2101 North Lincoln Boulevard, Room 480, Oklahoma City, OK 73105; (405) 521-2360.

OREGON

Race, color, religion, gender, national origin, marital status, age (if age eighteen or older), or juvenile record that has been expunged; protection is also extended to persons who associate with members of the protected groups: Fair Employment Act (Oreg. Rev. Stat. §659.030). Physical or mental disability (Oreg. Rev. Stat. §659.400). *Enforcing agency:* Civil Rights Division, Bureau of Labor and Industry, 800 N.E. Oregon Street, Box 32, Portland, OR 97232; (503) 731-4075.

PENNSYLVANIA

Race, color, religion, gender, national origin, ancestry, age (if between forty and seventy years old), physical or mental non-job-related handicap or disability, or use of a guide or support animal because of blindness, deafness, or physical handicap: Human Relations Act (43 Pa. Cons. Stat. Ann §954). *Enforcing agency:* Human Relations Commission, Uptown Shopping Plaza, 2971-E North 7th Street, Harrisburg, PA 17110-2123; (717) 787-4410.

RHODE ISLAND

Race, color, religion, gender, ancestry, age (if between forty and seventy years old), sexual orientation, or physical or mental disability: Fair Employment Practices Act (R.I. Gen. Laws §28-5-7). AIDS condition or the perception of it (R.I. Gen. Laws §23-6-22). *Enforcing agency:* Commission for Human Rights, 10 Abbott Park Place, Providence, RI 02903-3768; (401) 277-2661.

SOUTH CAROLINA

Race, color, religion, gender, age (if age forty or older), or national origin: Human Affairs Law (S.C. Code §1-13-20). Physical or mental disability (S.C. Code §43-33-530). *Enforcing agency:* Human Affairs Commission, 2611 Forest Drive, Suite 200, Columbia, SC 29204; (803) 253-6336.

SOUTH DAKOTA

Race, color, religion, creed, gender, national origin, ancestry, or physical and mental disability: Human Relations Act (S.Dak. Cod. Laws Ann. §20-13-10). *Enforcing agency:* Commission on Human Relations, 224 West Ninth Street, Sioux Falls, SD 57102; (605) 339-7039.

TENNESSEE

Race, creed, color, religion, gender, age (if age forty or older), or national origin: Fair Employment Practices Act (Tenn. Code Ann. §4-21-401). Physical or mental disability (Tenn. Code Ann. §8-50-103). *Enforcing agency:* Human Rights Commission, 531 Henley Street, Suite 701, Knoxville, TN 37902; (615) 594-6500.

TEXAS

Race, color, religion, gender, age (if between forty and seventy years old), national origin, or physical or mental disability: Commission on Human Rights Act (Vernon's Tex. Code Ann. Lab. §21.051). *Enforcing agency:* Commission on Human Rights, 8100 Cameron Road, Suite 525, Austin, TX 78754; (512) 837-8534.

UTAH

Race, color, religion, gender, age (if over age forty), national origin; pregnancy, childbirth, or related medical conditions; or physical or mental disability: Anti-Discrimination Act (Utah Code Ann. §§34-35-1 et seq.). *Enforcing agency:* Anti-Discrimination Division of the Industrial Commission, 160 East Third Street, South, 3rd floor, Salt Lake City, UT 84111; (801) 530-6801.

VERMONT

Race, color, religion, gender, national origin, ancestry, age (if age eighteen or older), place of birth, sexual orientation, HIV-positive condition, requiring a blood test for the presence of HIV, or physical or mental disability: Fair Employment Practices Act (Vt. Stat. Ann., t. 21, §§495 and 495a; t. 3, §961). *Enforcing agency:* Attorney General's Office, Civil Rights Division, 109 State Street, Montpelier, VT 05609; (802) 828-3657.

VIRGINIA

Race, color, religion, gender, national origin, age, marital status, or physical or mental disability: Human Rights Act (Va. Code Ann. §§2.1-714 et seq.). *Enforcing agency:* Council on Human Rights, 1100 Bank Street, Richmond, VA 23219; (804) 225-2292.

WASHINGTON

Race, color, creed, gender, age (if between forty and seventy years old), national origin, marital status; presence of any sensory, physical, or mental disability; or use of any trained guide or service dog by a disabled person (Wash. Rev. Code Ann. §49.60.180). *Enforcing agency:* Human Rights Commission, 1511 Third Avenue, Suite 921, Seattle, WA 98101; (206) 464-6500.

WEST VIRGINIA

Race, religion, color, national origin, gender, age (if age forty or older), or physical or mental disability: Human Rights Act (W.Va. Code §5-11-9). *Enforcing agency:* Human Rights Commission, 1321 Plaza East, Room 106, Charleston, WV 25301; (304) 348-6880.

WISCONSIN

Race, color, religion, gender, age (if age forty or older), national origin, sexual orientation, marital status, arrest or conviction record, or physical disability: Fair Employment Practices Act (Wis. Stat. Ann. §111.31). *Enforcing agency:* Department of Industry, Labor and Human Relations, Equal Rights Division, 201 East Washington Avenue, Room 402, Madison, WI 53708; (608) 266-6860.

WYOMING

Race, color, creed, gender, national origin, ancestry, age (if between forty and sixty-nine years old), or physical or mental disability: Fair Employment Practices Act (Wyo. Stat. §27-9-105). *Enforcing agency:* Fair Employment Commission, 6101 Yellowstone Street, Room 259C, Cheyenne, WY 82002; (307) 777-7262.

DRUG-FREE WORKPLACE

States not listed have no statute as of this writing.

ALABAMA

To qualify for a reduction in workers' compensation rates, you must require testing of all new hires and may perform tests on some applicants. You may test if there is a reasonable suspicion of illegal drug or alcohol use, may use regularly scheduled and random tests, and must test if the employee is involved in an injury-causing accident at the workplace. You must have an employee assistance program or provide a resource file on employee assistance programs (Ala. Code §§25-5-330 through 25-5-340).

CALIFORNIA

If you employ twenty-five or more people, you must reasonably accommodate any employee who enters an alcohol or drug rehabilitation program, unless the employee's current alcohol or drug use makes the employee unable to perform work duties or do a job safely. You're excused if this accommodation would impose an undue hardship on you. You must take reasonable efforts to safeguard the privacy of an employee who's enrolled in a treatment program (Calif. Lab. Code §§1025 and 1026).

CONNECTICUT

You may require a drug or alcohol test when there's a reasonable suspicion that an employee is under the influence and job performance is or could be impaired. You may test randomly when authorized by federal law, the employee works in a dangerous or safety-sensitive occupation, or the test is part of a voluntary employee assistance program. Job applicants may be required to submit to tests (Conn. Gen. Stat. §31-51t through 51aa).

FLORIDA

You may test for drugs and alcohol upon reasonable suspicion that an employee is under the influence, as a preemployment screening during routine fitness-for-duty examinations, and as a follow-up to participation in a drug treatment program (Fla. Stat. Ann. §440.101). Employees who voluntarily seek treatment for substance abuse can't be fired, disciplined, or discriminated against unless they've tested positive or have been in treatment in the past (Fla. Stat. Ann. §440.102).

GEORGIA

The state may not enter into any contract with a private contractor unless the contractor certifies that its workplace or site is drug-free. You must post your policy and report any employee convictions for illegal drug use to the state agency with which you've contracted. The statute doesn't establish drug testing by the employer (Ga. Code Ann. §50-24-1).

HAWAII

You may test employees or job applicants for substance abuse as long as the following conditions are met: you pay all costs; the test is performed by a licensed laboratory; the individuals tested are given a list of the substances they are being tested for and a disclosure form for the medicines and legal drugs they are taking; and the results are kept confidential (Hawaii Rev. Stat. §§329B-1 et seq.).

INDIANA

You may implement reasonable policies, including drug testing, designed to ensure that an employee is no longer using illegal drugs (Ind. Code §22-9-5-6).

IOWA

You can't request random drug testing of employees or require employees or job applicants to submit to a drug test as a condition of employment, preemployment, promotion, or change in employment status, except as part of a preemployment or regularly scheduled physical examination under certain restrictions. You may require a specific employee to submit to a drug test if there is a reasonable suspicion that the employee's faculties are impaired on the job or if the employee is in a position where such impairment presents a danger to the safety of others or if the impairment is a violation of one of your known rules (Iowa Code §730.5).

LOUISIANA

You may require all job applicants and employees to submit to drug testing as long as certain procedural guidelines are followed and the specimens are collected with due regard for the individual's privacy (La. Rev. Stat. Ann. §49:1001).

MAINE

You may require an employee to submit to a drug test when there is probable cause to believe the employee is impaired. Random testing is permitted when substance abuse might endanger coworkers or the public or when it is permitted by a union contract. Job applicants may be tested only if offered employment or placed on an eligibility roster (Maine Rev. Stat. Ann., t. 26, §§681–690).

MARYLAND

You may require testing of employees, contractors, or other people for job-related reasons for alcohol or drug abuse as long as certain procedural guidelines are followed (Md. Code Ann. Health Law §17-214.1).

MINNESOTA

You may require employees to submit to drug or alcohol testing if there is a written and posted testing policy and the test is performed by an independent licensed laboratory. Random tests may be given only to employees in "safety-sensitive" positions. Job applicants may be tested if they've been offered the job. Specific individuals may be tested when there is a reasonable suspicion that the employee is under the influence of drugs or alcohol; has violated a rule against use, possession, or distribution of drugs or alcohol on the job; or has caused an injury or accident at work (Minn. Stat. Ann. §§181.950 through 181.957) You may refuse to hire or may discipline or discharge an employee who refuses or fails to comply with the conditions established by a chemical dependency treatment or aftercare program (Minn. Stat. Ann. §§181.938(3) (4)).

MISSISSIPPI

You may require employees to submit to drug or alcohol testing if the policy is posted and certain prescribed procedures are followed. Testing is authorized when there is a reasonable suspicion that an employee is abusing drugs or alcohol. Random testing is also authorized. You may also test as part of routine fitness-for-duty examinations or as part of follow-up to a rehabilitation program. Job applicants may be tested if they're warned when they apply for the job (Miss. Code Ann. §§71-7 et seq.).

MONTANA

No person may be required to submit to a blood or urine test unless the job involves hazardous work or security, public safety, or fiduciary responsibilities (Mont. Code Ann. §39-2-304).

NEBRASKA

If you have more than six employees, you may require employees to submit to drug or alcohol testing if certain screening procedures are met. Refusal to undergo a test can be grounds for discipline or discharge (Nebr. Rev. Stat. §48-1901).

NORTH CAROLINA

You may test applicants and employees for the presence of controlled substances as long as you follow specified procedures, including the preservation of the test sample so that the applicant or employee may perform his or her own test (N.C. Gen. Stat. §§95-230 through 235).

OKLAHOMA

You may test applicants and employees as long as you adhere to statutory procedures and issue a written workplace policy. An applicant may be tested as long as all applicants are tested; an employee may be tested if you have a reasonable suspicion that the employee has violated the written policy. Random testing is allowed for certain employees only, including those whose jobs directly affect the safety of others: Standards for Workplace Drug and Alcohol Testing Act (Okla. Stat. Ann., t. 40, §§551–565).

OREGON

You may not require any employee or job applicant to submit to any Breathalyzer alcohol test unless there is a reasonable suspicion that the employee is under the influence of alcohol (Oreg. Rev. Stat. §659-227). Employees may be required to be tested for drugs if the laboratory used is licensed by the state and certain procedural safeguards are employed (Oreg. Rev. Stat. §438-435).

RHODE ISLAND

You may require employees to submit to drug or alcohol testing when there is reason to believe that the use of controlled substances is impairing the employee's ability to do the job, the test sample is provided in private, the testing is part of a rehabilitation program, positive results are confirmed by the most accurate method available, the employee is given reasonable notice that the test will be given, and the employee is given a chance to explain the results (R.I. Gen. Laws §28-6.5-1).

UTAH

If you test for drugs, you must have a written policy regarding the methods used, and management must submit to regular testing as well as employees. A positive test result may be used as grounds for suspension, discipline, or discharge. Employees who test positive are not to be considered "handicapped" under the state's antidiscrimination law (Utah Code Ann. §§34-38-1 through 15).

VERMONT

You may require employees to be tested for drugs or alcohol if there is a probable cause to believe the employee is using or is under the influence on the job, the employer provides a rehabilitation program, and the employee who tests positive is given a chance to participate in the rehabilitation program rather than being fired. Employees who have already been through rehabilitation and who again test positive may be fired. Job applicants may be tested when they have been offered the job conditioned on passing the test, if they are given advance notice of the test and the test is given as part of a comprehensive physical examination. Applicants and employees must be given the opportunity to retest a sample that has tested positive (Vt. Stat. Ann., t. 21, §511).

FAMILY AND MEDICAL LEAVE

Many states guarantee employees the right to take work leaves because of pregnancy, childbirth, or the adoption of a child. Some have laws that give employees the right to take time off from work to care for a family member who is ill. States not appearing on this list have no statute as of this writing.

ALASKA

If you employ twenty-one or more people, you must grant any employee who has worked full time for six months or half time for one year eighteen weeks of unpaid leave per twelve-month period for pregnancy, childbirth, or adoption or twenty-four months for care of a family member during a serious illness. Employees who take such leave must be restored to their same or comparable position (Alaska Stat. §23.10.500).

CALIFORNIA

You must grant a leave of up to four months for a female employee who is disabled as a result of pregnancy, childbirth, or related medical conditions (Calif. Govt. Code §12945). Employees who have worked for at least one year and have 1,250 hours of work during the previous year may take up to twelve working weeks in any twelve-month period for family care and medical leave, with reemployment guaranteed. This applies only if you employ fifty people or more; it does not apply if you employ fewer than fifty people within seventy-five miles of the employee's work site (Calif. Govt. Code §1245.2.). If you employ twenty-five or more people at the same location, you must grant parents, guardians, or custodial grandparents up to forty hours per school year of unpaid time off (but not more that eight hours per calendar month) to participate in school activities of a child in grades kindergarten through twelve, as long as the employee gives reasonable advance notice. You may require verification from the school (Calif. Lab. Code §230.8). You may not discharge or discriminate against an employee who is called to attend a child's school following a suspension. The employee must give reasonable advance notice (Calif. Lab. Code §230.7).

COLORADO

Your policies applying to leaves for biological parents must also extend to adoptive parents (Colo. Rev. Stat. §19-5-211).

CONNECTICUT

If you employ at least seventy-five people, you must give sixteen weeks of unpaid leave within any two-year period. Leave may be for birth or adoption of a child or for care of a child, spouse, or parent during serious illness. Employees who take such leave must be allowed to return to either their original or equivalent jobs (Conn. Gen. Stat. §§31-51cc, 31-51dd, and 31-51ff).

DISTRICT OF COLUMBIA

If you employ at least twenty people, an employee who has worked with your company for at least one year and who has worked at least 1,000 hours during the previous twelve-month period must be granted up to sixteen weeks of unpaid leave during any twenty-four-month period in connection with the birth or adoption of a child or serious illness of a family member (D.C. Code Ann. §36-1302). "Family member" includes a child who lives with the employee and for whom the employee assumes parental responsibility. It also includes a person with whom the employee shares and maintains a residence. Employees who take such leaves must be restored to either their original or equivalent jobs.

HAWAII

If you employ at least one hundred people, you must grant them an unpaid leave of up to four weeks per calendar year for the birth or adoption of a child or for care of a child, spouse, or parent during a serious illness. Employees who take such leave must be restored to their same or comparable positions (Hawaii Rev. Stat. §§398-1 through 11).

ILLINOIS

You must give employees up to eight hours during each school year to attend a child's classroom activities and conferences that cannot be scheduled during nonwork hours. The employee must first exhaust all vacation and compensatory time and must give you seven days' notice except in an emergency (820 Ill. Comp. Stat. 147/15).

IOWA

If you employ at least four people, you must grant employees who are disabled by pregnancy, childbirth, or related medical conditions an unpaid leave for the duration of their disabilities, up to a maximum of eight weeks (Iowa Code Ann. §216.6).

KENTUCKY

You must grant up to six weeks of unpaid leave to an employee who has adopted a child under seven years old (Ky. Rev. Stat. Ann. §337.015).

LOUISIANA

You must give an employee up to six weeks of leave and must grant an additional leave for a "reasonable period of time" not to exceed four months (La. Rev. Stat. Ann. §22:215.7). You may grant up to sixteen unpaid hours per year for an employee to attend or participate in school conferences and activities of a child for whom the employee is the legal guardian, if those activities can't be scheduled during nonwork hours. The employee must give reasonable notice and schedule the time off so that it does not unduly disrupt your operations (La. Rev. Stat. Ann. §23:1015).

MAINE

If you employ at least twenty-five people at the work site, an employee who has worked at least twelve consecutive months at your company must be granted up to ten consecutive weeks of unpaid leave in any two-year period for the birth or adoption of a child under sixteen years old or to care for a family member during illness. Employees who take such leaves must be restored to either their original or equivalent jobs (Maine Rev. Stat. Ann., t. 26, §844).

MASSACHUSETTS

If you employ at least six people, you must grant employees who have completed their probationary periods or have worked full time for at least three months up to eight weeks of unpaid leave for the birth or adoption of a child under eighteen or the adoption of a child under twenty-three if the child is mentally or physically disabled (Mass. Gen. Law Ann., ch. 149, §105D).

MINNESOTA

If you employ twenty-one or more people, you must grant employees up to six weeks of unpaid leave for the birth or adoption of a child. However, only employees who have worked for your company an average of at least twenty hours per week for at least twelve months before the request for leave is made are covered. During the leave, you must offer the employee the option of continuing group health insurance coverage. Employees who take such leaves must be returned to either their original or equivalent jobs, unless they would have been laid off (Minn. Stat. Ann. §181.941). An employee may use paid sick leave to care for a sick child (Minn. Stat. Ann. §181.943). You must grant up to forty hours with pay to enable an employee to donate bone marrow (Minn. Stat. Ann. §181.945). An employee is entitled to sixteen hours of paid leave per year to attend school conferences or classroom activities that can't be scheduled during nonwork hours (Minn. Stat. Ann. §181.9412).

MONTANA

You may not dismiss an employee who becomes pregnant, refuse to allow a reasonable unpaid leave for pregnancy, or refuse to allow accrued disability or other leave benefits for a pregnancy leave. Employees also cannot be required to take pregnancy leave for an unreasonable period of time. Employees who take pregnancy-related leaves must be returned to their original jobs or equivalent unless your business's circumstances have changed so as to make it unreasonable or impossible to do so (Mont. Code Ann §§49-2-310 and 49-2-311).

NEVADA

The same leave policies that apply to other medical conditions must be extended to female employees before and after childbirth or after a miscarriage (Nev. Rev. Stat. §613.335).

NEW JERSEY

If you employ at least fifty people, you must grant to those who have worked for at least twelve months and who have worked at least 1,000 hours in the preceding twelve months up to twelve weeks of unpaid leave in any twenty-four-month period for the birth, adoption, or care during the serious illness of a child under eighteen years old, one older than eighteen who is incapable of self-care, a parent, or a spouse. Employees who take such leaves must be restored to either their original or equivalent jobs. You may deny leave if the employee is among the seven highest-paid employees or among the top 5 percent in pay, whichever is greater, and if substantial and grievous economic injury to the business would result. You must notify the employee of your intent to deny leave when you determine that denial is necessary. If leave has commenced, the employee must return within ten days: Family Leave Act (N.J. Stat. Ann. §§34:11B-1 through B16).

NEW YORK

If you permit leave for the birth of a child, you must grant leave for adoption (N.Y. Lab. Law §201-c). You must grant employee up to twenty-four hours of leave to donate bone marrow and may not retaliate against an employee who requests a leave for this purpose (N.Y. Lab. Law §202-a).

NORTH CAROLINA

An employee who is a parent, guardian, or acting parent may take up to four hours per year without pay to be involved in the child's school (public or private school or day care). The hours taken must be at a mutually agreed time; you may require forty-eight hours' notice for the request and may require verification that the employee actually attended or was involved. You may not retaliate against an employee who exercises rights under this law (N.C. Stat. §95-28.3).

OREGON

If you employ at least twenty-five people, employees who have worked with your company for at least ninety days must be granted up to twelve weeks of unpaid leave for childbirth or the adoption of a child less than six years old. You may require employees to give thirty days' notice of their intent to take such a leave, and employees returning from such a leave must be returned to either their original or equivalent jobs. Pregnant employees must also be given the right to transfer to less strenuous jobs (Oreg. Rev. Stat. §659.360). If you have fifty or more employees, you must grant to employees who have worked an average of at least twenty-four hours per week for 180 days or more a leave of absence to care for a seriously ill family member of up to twelve weeks in a two-year period (Oreg. Rev. Stat. §659.570).

RHODE ISLAND

If you employ fifty or more people, you must grant those who have worked with you for at least twelve consecutive months up to thirteen weeks of unpaid leave in any two calendar years for the birth or adoption of a child or for the care of a family member during illness. Employees who take such leaves must be restored to either their original or equivalent jobs (R.I. Gen. Laws §§28-48-2 and 28-48-3).

TENNESSEE

If you employ one hundred or more people, you must grant up to four months of unpaid leave for pregnancy or childbirth to any full-time female employee who has worked at least twelve consecutive months. If the employee gives you at least three months' advance notice of her intent to take such a leave or if a medical emergency makes the leave necessary, she must be restored to her original job or its equivalent upon returning to work. You must allow an employee who takes such a leave to continue benefits such as health insurance, but you're not required to pay for the benefits during the leave period. If the employee's job is "so unique" that you can't, with reasonable efforts, fill the position temporarily, you need not reinstate the employee. Reinstatement rights don't apply if the employee uses the time to pursue other employment opportunities or has worked full time or part time for another employer (Tenn. Code Ann. §4-21-408).

VERMONT

If you employ fifteen or more people, you must allow those who have worked an average of at least thirty hours per week for at least one year to take up to twelve weeks of unpaid leave per year for pregnancy, childbirth, the adoption of a child under the age of sixteen, or the serious illness of the employee or a family member. The employee must provide you with written notice of the intent to take such a leave and of its anticipated duration. The employee must be allowed to use accrued vacation or sickness leave for up to six weeks of leave. The employee must also be given the option of continuing benefit programs at his or her own expense. After returning from such a leave, the employee must be restored to the original job or its equivalent, unless you can demonstrate that the employee performed unique services and hiring a permanent replacement worker, after giving notice to the employee, was the only alternative to preventing substantial and grievous economic injury to your business. An employee who doesn't return to the job after taking such a leave for reasons other than his or her serious illness must refund to you any compensation paid during the leave, except payments for accrued vacation or sickness leave (Vt. Stat. Ann., t. 21, §472).

WASHINGTON

If you employ one hundred or more people, you must grant up to twelve weeks of unpaid leave during any two-year period in connection with the birth or adoption of a child or to care for a child under the age of eighteen who is terminally ill. The employee must give you at least thirty days' advance notice in most situations. Employees who take such leaves must be restored to their original or equivalent jobs. If circumstances have changed to the point that no equivalent job is available, the employee must be given any vacant job for which he or she is qualified. You may limit or deny family leave to either the highest-paid 10 percent of the employees or 10 percent designated as "key" personnel (Wash. Rev. Code §49.12.270).

WISCONSIN

If you employ fifty or more people, you must grant employees who have been with your company one year and worked 1,000 hours up to six weeks of unpaid leave for the birth or adoption of a child and up to two weeks for the care of a parent, child, or spouse with a serious health condition. This leave, when combined with any other family-related leave, may not exceed a total of eight weeks within a twelve-month period (Wis. Stat. Ann. §103.10).

INSURANCE CONTINUATION

Here is a quick view of state laws that give employees the right to continue group health insurance after leaving the employment of the company sponsoring the insurance. States not appearing on this list have no statute as of this writing.

ARKANSAS

Former employees and their dependents have the right to continue group insurance coverage for 120 days after the coverage would have ended because of a change in employment status (Ark. Stat. Ann. §23-86-114).

CALIFORNIA

Former employees and their dependents, including widows and widowers and divorced spouses, have the right to continue group insurance coverage for ninety days after termination (Calif. Health & Safety Code §§1373.62 and 1373.6).

COLORADO

Former employees who were terminated and had been covered for at least three months by group health insurance and their dependents have the right to continue that coverage ninety days or until reemployed, whichever comes first (Colo. Rev. Stat. §10-8-116).

CONNECTICUT

Former employees and their eligible dependents have the right to continue group health insurance for seventy-eight weeks after the coverage would have ended or until they are covered by another group plan, whichever comes first (Conn. Gen. Stat. §38-262d).

FLORIDA

Former employees who were terminated and had been covered by group health insurance for at least three months and their eligible dependents have the right to covert the coverage to an individual policy (Fla. Stat. §627.6675).

GEORGIA

Former employees and their eligible dependents who have been covered by group health insurance have the right to continue coverage for three months after the end of employment (Ga. Code Ann. §33-24-21.1).

ILLINOIS

Former employees who were terminated and had been covered by group health insurance for at least three months have the right to continue group coverage unless they are covered by another group plan (Ill. Stat. Ann., ch. 73, §979e).

IOWA

Former employees who were terminated have the right to continue group health insurance for nine months, but some types of coverage, such as prescription drug benefits, are excluded (Iowa Code Ann. §509b.3).

KANSAS

Former employees have the right to continue group health insurance for six months after the end of employment (Kans. Stat. Ann. §40-2209).

KENTUCKY

Former employees who had been covered by group health insurance for at least three months have the right to continue that coverage for nine months (Ky. Rev. Stat. Ann. §304.18-110).

LOUISIANA

A former employee's surviving spouse who is fifty years old or older can continue group health coverage (La. Civ. Code Ann., art. 22, §215.7).

MAINE

Former employees who have been covered by group health insurance for six months and have been terminated because of layoff or work-related injury or occupational disease can continue group coverage (Maine Rev. Stat. Ann., t. 24-A, §2809-A).

MARYLAND

Former employees who were involuntarily terminated and had been covered by group health insurance for at least three months have the right to continue that coverage (Md. Ann. Code, art. 48A, §§354FF, 477GG, 477K, and 490G).

MASSACHUSETTS

Former employees and their dependents may continue group health insurance for thirty-one days. If employment was terminated by plant closing, insurance may be continued for ninety days. If employment ended by layoff or death, insurance may be continued for thirty-nine weeks (Mass. Gen. Laws Ann., ch. 175, §110G; ch. 176A, §8D; ch. 176B, §6A; ch. 176G, §4A).

MINNESOTA

Former employees who quit or were terminated for reasons other than gross misconduct have the right to continue group health coverage for themselves and their families for twelve months after it would otherwise end or until they become covered by another group plan, whichever comes first (Minn. Stat. Ann. §62A.17).

MISSOURI

Former employees who have been covered by a group health plan for at least three months have the right to continue that insurance for up to nine months after it would otherwise end (Mo. Ann. Stat. §376.428).

NEBRASKA

Former employees are entitled to continue group health insurance for six months after employment ends unless termination was due to employee misconduct (Nebr. Rev. Stat. §44-1633).

NEVADA

Former employees who have been covered by a group health plan for at least three months are entitled to continue coverage for eighteen months unless terminated for misconduct. Eligible dependents are entitled to continue coverage for thirty-six months. No coverage if employee voluntarily quits (Nev. Rev. Stat. Ann. §§689B.245 and 689b.246).

NEW HAMPSHIRE

Former employees and eligible dependents are entitled to continuation of group health coverage if employee is terminated or dies, unless the termination is for misconduct or is for less that six months. Coverage continues for twenty-nine months if termination is due to disability, thirty-six months for spouse upon separation or divorce or if employee dies, and eighteen months in all other situations (N.H. Rev. Stat. Ann. §415.18).

NEW JERSEY

Former employees are entitled to continuation of group health coverage if termination is due to total disability and they have been covered for three months (N.J. Stat. Ann. §17B:27-51-12).

NEW MEXICO

Former employees have the right to continue group health insurance coverage for up to six months after it would otherwise end. Covered family members may convert to individual policies upon the former employee's death or divorce (N.Mex. Stat. Ann. §59-18-16(A)).

NEW YORK

Former employees have the right to continue group health coverage for up to six months after date of termination (N.Y. Ins. Law §3221).

NORTH CAROLINA

Former employees and their eligible dependents are entitled to continue group health plan coverage for three months if they have been covered by the plan for at least three months (N.C. Gen. Stat. §58-53-35).

NORTH DAKOTA

Former employees who had been covered by group health insurance for at least three months have the right to continue that coverage (N.Dak. Cent. Code §26.1-36-23).

OHIO

Former employees who were terminated involuntarily have the right to continue group health insurance coverage for six months after termination (Ohio Rev. Code. Ann. §1737.30).

OKLAHOMA

Former employees are entitled to continue group health coverage for thirty days after termination. If the employee has been covered by the plan for at least six months and is suffering from a continuing medical condition, basic medical coverage continues for three months and major medical coverage continues for six months (Okla. Stat. Ann., t. 40, §§172 and 173).

OREGON

Former employees and eligible dependents who have been covered by a group health insurance plan for at least three months are entitled to continuation of coverage for six months after the end of employment (Oreg. Rev. Stat. §742.850).

RHODE ISLAND

Former employees who were terminated due to an involuntary layoff or death have the right to continue group health insurance coverage for themselves and their dependents for up to eighteen months after it would otherwise end (R.I. Gen. Laws §27-19.1-1).

SOUTH CAROLINA

Former employees who have been covered by a group health plan for at least three months are entitled to continue coverage after employment ends for one month (S.C. Code Ann. §38-45-946).

SOUTH DAKOTA

Former employees and their dependents who have been covered by a group health insurance plan for at least six months have the right to continue that coverage for up to eighteen months after it would otherwise end (S.Dak. Cod. Laws Ann. §58-18-7.5).

TENNESSEE

Former employees who had been covered by group health insurance for at least three months have the right to continue that coverage for up to three months after it would otherwise end. The employee is required to pay the premium in advance (Tenn. Code Ann. §56-7-1501).

TEXAS

Former employees who have been covered by a group health insurance plan for at least three months and who are not terminated for cause are entitled to continue coverage for six months (Tex. Rev. Civ. Stat. Ann., art. 3.51-6).

UTAH

Former employees who have been covered by a group health insurance plan for at least six months are entitled to continue coverage for two months after end of employment (Utah Code Ann. §31A-22-703).

VERMONT

Former employees who have been covered by a group health insurance plan for at least three months are entitled to continue such coverage unless terminated for misconduct (Vt. Stat. Ann., t. 3, §§4090a through 4090g).

VIRGINIA

Former employees who have been covered by a group health insurance plan for at least three months may either continue coverage for ninety days after employment ends or convert to an individual policy at the employer's option (Va. Code Ann. §38.2-1541).

WASHINGTON

Former employees are entitled to continue group health insurance benefits for a period of time and at a rate that employer and employee have agreed on (Wash. Rev. Code Ann. §§48.21.250 through 48.21.270).

WEST VIRGINIA

Former employees who have been involuntarily laid off are entitled to continue group health benefits for eighteen months (W.Va. Code §33-16-3).

WISCONSIN

Former employees who have been covered by group health insurance for at least three months have the right to continue coverage or convert it to an individual policy, unless they were fired for misconduct. If the former employee chooses group coverage, it will continue indefinitely and cannot be terminated unless the former employee moves out of state or becomes eligible for similar coverage (Wis. Stat. §632.897).

MEAL AND REST PERIODS

States not appearing here have no statute as of this writing.

ALABAMA

You can't require an employee who is fifteen years old or younger to work five continuous hours without a meal or rest break of at least thirty minutes (Ala. Code §25-8-38 (c)).

ARKANSAS

If your workplace has more than six employees, you must provide a separate lunchroom for the women. If this is impracticable, you must give female employees at least one hour for lunch and permit them to leave your establishment (Ark. Code. Ann. §11-5-112)

CALIFORNIA

Meal: Thirty minutes within five hours of starting work if workday is six hours or more; if less, waivable. *Rest:* Ten minutes per four-hour period; compensated: Industrial Welfare Commission Order No. 1-89. (Does not apply to motion picture, agricultural, and household occupations.)

COLORADO

Meal: Thirty minutes within five hours of starting work; optional if workday is not over six hours. *Rest:* Ten minutes per four hours (Wage Order No. 19).

CONNECTICUT

Meal: Thirty minutes per 7.5-hour workday; must be given after the second hour and before the final two hours (Gen. Stat. §31-51ii).

DELAWARE

Meal: Thirty minutes per 7.5-hour workday; must be given after the second hour and before the final two hours (Del. Code Ann., t. 19, §707).

ILLINOIS

Meal: Twenty minutes for a 7.5-hour workday beginning no later than five hours into the work period (830 Ill. Comp. Stat. 140/3).

IOWA

Employees under the age of sixteen who work five or more hours are entitled to a thirty-minute break (Iowa Code §92.7).

KENTUCKY

Meal: "Reasonable" meal break between three and five hours into the work period. *Rest:* Ten minutes per four hours (Ky. Rev. Stat. Ann. §§337.355 and 337.365). Statute does not apply to railroad employees.

LOUISIANA

Divers, tunnel, and caisson workers who use compressed air must be given open-air rest intervals between shifts as specified in the statute (La. Rev. Stat. Ann. §23:486).

MAINE

Thirty minutes per six hours of work for meals or rest (Maine Rev. Stat. Ann., t. 26, §§601 and 602).

MASSACHUSETTS

Meal: Thirty minutes per six-hour work period (Mass. Gen. Laws Ann., ch. 149, §100).

MICHIGAN

Minors who are employed more than five continuous hours must be given thirty minutes for a meal or rest break (Mich. Comp. Laws §17.731(12)).

MINNESOTA

Meal: Employer must allow "adequate time" to eat a meal during an eight-hour work period (Minn. Stat. Ann. §177.254).

NEBRASKA

All employees in assembly plants, workshops, or mechanical establishments are required to have at least thirty-minute lunch breaks between noon and 1:00 p.m. without having to remain on the premises unless the plant operates twenty-four hours per day (Nebr. Rev. Stat. §48-212).

NEVADA

Meal: Thirty minutes per eight hours of work. *Rest:* Ten minutes per four hours of work (Nev. Rev. Stat. Ann. §608.019).

NEW HAMPSHIRE

Meal: Thirty minutes per five hours of work, except if it is feasible for the employee to eat while working and the employer allows him or her to do so (N.H. Rev. Stat. Ann §275:30-a).

NEW MEXICO

Women's working hours are restricted to eight hours per day and forty-eight hours per week, except for domestic workers and workers in interstate commerce. Those employees must be given a thirty-minute rest period, which is not counted as part of the working day (N.Mex. Stat. Ann. §50-5-4).

NEW YORK

Meal: Thirty minutes at mercantile or similar establishments; sixty minutes at factories. If shift begins before 11:00 a.m. and extends past 7:00 p.m., an additional twenty minutes must be given to factory and mercantile workers between 5:00 p.m. and 7:00 p.m. If shift is more than six hours long and begins between 1:00 p.m. and 6:00 a.m., mercantile employees are to receive forty-five minutes and factory employees sixty minutes at a point midway through the shift (N.Y. Lab. Law §162).

NORTH DAKOTA

Meal: Thirty minutes if shift is over five hours; by wage order. Commissioner of Labor sets the standards (N.Dak. Cent. Code §34-06-03).

OREGON

Meal: Thirty minutes for each work period of between six and eight hours within the second and fifth hour worked. Or if work period is more than seven hours, break to be given between the third and sixth hour worked. *Rest:* Ten minutes for every four hours worked (Oreg. Admin. Rules §839-020-050).

RHODE ISLAND

Meal: Twenty minutes per six hours of work (R.I. Gen. Laws §28-3-14).

TENNESSEE

Meal: Thirty unpaid minutes for a six-hour work period, except if your workplace by its nature provides for ample opportunity to rest or take an appropriate break (Tenn. Code Ann. §50-2-103).

VIRGINIA

Any county having the county manager form of organization may establish laws regulating hours and conditions of employment (Va. Code §15.1-658).

WEST VIRGINIA

Meal: Twenty minutes (W.Va. Admin. Reg. §42-5-2.6).

WISCONSIN

Meal: Thirty minutes close to usual mealtime or near middle of shift. Shifts or more than six hours without a meal break should be avoided. Break mandatory for minors (Wis. Admin. Code, ind. 74.02).

WYOMING

You must give women employees two rest periods of not less than fifteen minutes, one before the lunch hour and one after lunch, if the employees are required to be on their feet continuously (Wyo. Stat. Ann. §27-6-101).

MINIMUM WAGE

States not listed here have no statute at the time of this writing.

ALASKA

Fifty cents above federal minimum wage (Alaska Stat. §23.10.065).

ARKANSAS

$4.25 per hour (Ark. Code Ann. §11-4-210)

CALIFORNIA

Not less than the federal minimum wage (Calif. Lab. Code §1182).

COLORADO

$4.25 per hour by order of the Labor Division (Colo. Rev. Stat. §§8-6-109, 8-6-110, and 8-6-111).

CONNECTICUT

$4.27 per hour, or at least 0.5 percent above the federal minimum wage, whichever is higher (Conn. Gen. Stat. §31-58j).

DELAWARE

The federal minimum wage (Del. Code Ann., t. 19, §902a).

DISTRICT OF COLUMBIA

Federal minimum wage plus $1 per hour (D.C. Code Ann. §§36-220.1 and 36-220.2).

FLORIDA

If a manual laborer is paid by the day, week, or month, ten hours constitutes a day's work. Hours worked in excess entitle the employee to extra pay unless you and the employee have otherwise agreed by contract (Fla. Stat. §448.01).

GEORGIA

$3.25 per hour (Ga. Code Ann. §34-4-3a).

HAWAII

$5.25 per hour (Hawaii Rev. Stat. §387-2).

IDAHO

$4.25 per hour (Idaho Code §44-1502).

ILLINOIS

$4.25 per hour (820 Ill. Comp. Stat. 105/4).

INDIANA

$3.35 per hour if you employ at least two employees (Ind. Code Ann. §22-2-2-4).

IOWA

$4.65 per hour (Iowa Code Ann. §91D.1).

KANSAS

$2.65 per hour (Kans. Stat. Ann. §44-1203).

KENTUCKY

$4.25 per hour (Ky. Rev. Stat. Ann §337.275).

LOUISIANA

The secretary of the Department of Transportation and Development must establish a subsistence salary for employees who must spend workdays away from their usual place of residence (La. Rev. Stat. Ann. §48:53).

MAINE

Same as federal minimum wage up to $5.00 per hour (Maine Rev. Stat. Ann., t. 26, §664).

MARYLAND

Not less than the federal minimum wage (Md. Code Ann., Lab. & Empl., §3-413).

MASSACHUSETTS

$5.75, unless the commissioner approves a lesser wage (Mass. Gen. Law Ann., ch. 151, §1).

MICHIGAN

$3.35 per hour (Mich. Stat. Ann. §17.255(4)).

MINNESOTA

$4.25 per hour for employers grossing more than $362,500 per year; $4.00 per hour for others (Minn. Stat. Ann. §177.24).

MISSISSIPPI

$4.25 per hour; set by the Employment Security Commission. Participants in the Work First Program must be paid the federal or state minimum wage, whichever is higher (Miss. Code Ann. §43-49-11).

MISSOURI

The federal minimum wage (Mo. Ann. Stat. §290.502).

MONTANA

$4.25 per hour for businesses with gross annual sales of $110.00 or more; $4.00 per hour for others (Mont. Code Ann. §§39-3-404 and 39-3-409; Dept. Lab. Ind. Rules §24.16.15104).

NEBRASKA

$4.25 per hour (Nebr. Rev. Stat. §48-1203).

NEVADA

$4.25 per hour (Notice of the Labor Commissioner, April 1, 1991).

NEW HAMPSHIRE

Federal minimum wage or the state minimum wage (currently $3.95), whichever is higher (N.H. Rev. Stat. Ann. §279:21).

NEW JERSEY

$5.05 per hour (N.J. Stat. Ann. §34:11-56a4).

NEW MEXICO

$4.25 per hour (N.Mex. Stat. Ann. §50-4-22).

NEW YORK

$4.25 per hour (N.Y. Lab. Law §652).

NORTH CAROLINA

$4.25 per hour (N.C. Gen. Stat. §95-25.3).

NORTH DAKOTA

$4.25 per hour. Commissioner of labor sets the standards of minimum wages, hours of employment, and conditions of employment (N.Dak. Cent. Code §34-06-03).

OHIO

$4.25 per hour (Ohio Rev. Code Ann. §4111.02).

OKLAHOMA

Not less than current federal minimum wage (Okla. Stat. Ann., t. 40, §197.2).

OREGON

$4.75 per hour (Oreg. Rev. Stat. §653.025).

PENNSYLVANIA

The federal minimum wage (Pa. Cons. Stat. Ann §333.104).

RHODE ISLAND

$4.45 per hour (R.I. Gen. Laws §28-12-3).

SOUTH DAKOTA

$4.25 per hour (S.Dak. Cod. Laws Ann. §60-11-3).

TEXAS

$3.35 per hour, but you are allowed to pay as little as 60 percent of the minimum wage if the employee's earning or productive capacity is impaired by age, physical or mental deficiency, or injury or if the employee is over sixty-five years old. Lower wages may not be paid to agricultural piece-rate workers (Lab. Code Ann. §§62.051, 62.055, and 62.057).

UTAH

$4.25 per hour for employees eighteen and older; does not apply to waiting on tables. Set by the Industrial Commission of Utah but may not be more than the federal minimum wage (Utah Code Ann. §34-40-103).

VERMONT

$4.75 per hour or the federal minimum wage, whichever is higher (Vt. Stat. Ann., t. 21, §384a).

VIRGINIA

Not less than the federal minimum wage (Va. Code Ann. §40.1-28.10).

WASHINGTON

$4.90 per hour (Wash. Rev. Code Ann. §49.46.020).

WEST VIRGINIA

$4.25 per hour (W.Va. Code §21-5C-2a).

WISCONSIN

$4.25 per hour; $3.90 for employees under the age of eighteen. Set by wage order of the Dept. of Industry, Labor and Human Relations Regulations (Wis. Stat. Ann. §104.02).

WYOMING

$1.60 per hour (Wyo. Stat. §27-4-202).

PERSONNEL FILES

States not listed here have no statute at the time of this writing.

ALABAMA

Employees have the right to see their personnel files and make a copy of them (Ala. Stat. §23.10.430).

CALIFORNIA

Employees have the right to receive a copy of any employment-related document they've signed (Calif. Lab. Code §432). You must maintain a copy of the employee's personnel file where the employee reports to work or must make the file available at that location within a reasonable time after the employee asks to see it. Statute does not apply to letters of reference or records relating to the investigation of a possible offense (Calif. Lab. Code §1198.5).

CONNECTICUT

Employees have the right to see their personnel files and to insert rebuttals of information with which they disagree (Conn. Gen. Stat. Ann. §31-128b).

DELAWARE

Employees have the right to see their personnel files and to insert rebuttals of information with which they disagree (Del. Code Ann., t. 19, §§730 through 735).

ILLINOIS

If you employ five or more people, you must allow them to see their personnel files and to insert rebuttals of any information with which they disagree: Personnel Record Review Act (820 Ill. Rev. Stat. 40/0. DI).

IOWA

Employees have the right to see and copy personnel files, including performance evaluations and disciplinary records but not letters of reference (Iowa Code §91B.1).

LOUISIANA

Current or former employees, or their designated representatives, have a right of access to your records of employee exposure, medical records, and analyses using employee records (La. Rev. Stat. Ann. §23.1016).

MAINE

Employees have the right to see and make copies of their personnel files, including workplace evaluations (Maine Rev. Stat. Ann., t. 26, §631).

MASSACHUSETTS

Employees have the right to see their personnel files and to insert rebuttals of any information with which they disagree. Employees may take court action to expunge from personnel records any information that the employer knows, or should have known, was incorrect. Statute does not apply to employees of private institutions of higher learning who are tenured, on tenure track, or have similar positions or responsibilities (Mass. Gen. Laws Ann., ch. 149, §52c).

MICHIGAN

Employees have the right to see and make a copy of their personnel files and to insert rebuttals of any information with which they disagree. Access isn't available to employees you're investigating for criminal activity that may cause loss to your business. Upon completion of the investigation or after two years, whichever comes first, you must tell the employee of the outcome, and if no disciplinary action is taken, you must destroy the investigation file (Mich. Comp. Laws §§17(62) et seq.).

MINNESOTA

If you employ twenty or more people, they have the right to see their personnel files and to insert rebuttals of any information with which they disagree. A former employee may inspect his or her file once within the year following termination. You may not use in any retaliatory way any information intentionally left out of the personnel record (Minn. Stat. Ann. §§181.960 through 181.965).

NEVADA

Employees who have been employed at least sixty days have the right to see and copy any records that you used to confirm the employee's qualifications or as the basis for any disciplinary action. If those records contain incorrect information, the employee may notify you of the errors in writing. You're required to correct the challenged information if you decide it's false. The employee can't inspect confidential reports from past employers or reports from an investigative agency regarding the employee's violation of any law (Nev. Rev. Stat. §613.075).

NEW HAMPSHIRE

Employees have the right to see and copy their personnel files and to insert rebuttals of any information that relates to a government security investigation or information regarding an investigation of the employee if that disclosure would prejudice law enforcement (N.H. Rev. Stat. §275:56).

OREGON

Employees have the right to see and copy any documents you used in making work-related decisions, such as promotions, wage increases, or termination (Oreg. Rev. Stat. §652.750).

PENNSYLVANIA

Employers and their designated agents have the right to see their personnel files. The files may not be copied or removed (Pa. Cons. Stat. Ann., t. 43, §§1321 through 1325).

RHODE ISLAND

Employees have the right to see their personnel files up to three times per year. A file may not be copied or removed, but an employee may request that specific documents be copied (R.I. Gen. Laws §§28-6.4-1 and 28-6.4-2).

WASHINGTON

Employees have the right to see their personnel files and to insert rebuttals of any information with which they disagree. A former employee retains the right of rebuttal or correction for two years. Does not apply if the employee is subject to criminal investigation or if the records have been compiled in preparation for an impending lawsuit (Wash. Rev. Code. §§49.12.240 through 49.12.260).

WISCONSIN

Employees have the right to see and copy their personnel files up to twice a year and to insert rebuttals of any information with which they disagree. The rebuttal must be attached to the record and transmitted with it to any third party. Does not apply if employee is subject to a criminal investigation, to references or recommendations, or to records subject to a pending claim in a judicial proceeding. Personnel records include medical records, but if you think that disclosure of these would be detrimental to the employee, you may instead disclose them to a physician designated by the employee (Wis. Stat. §103.13).

TERMINATION AND PAY

State provisions specify how soon a final paycheck must be given to an employee. States not listed have no applicable provisions at the time of this writing.

ALASKA

Within three days (Alaska Stat. §23.05.140).

ARIZONA

If you are fired: within three days or next scheduled payday; if you quit: next scheduled payday (Ariz. Rev. Stat. Ann. §23-353).

ARKANSAS

If you are fired: within seven days after your demand; if you quit: no applicable law (Ark. Code §11-4-405).

CALIFORNIA

If you are fired: immediately or within seventy-two hours for employees of the seasonal industries; if you quit: within seventy-two hours or immediately if you have given seventy-two hours' notice (Calif. Lab. Code §§201 and 202).

COLORADO

If you are fired: immediately; if you quit: next scheduled payday (Colo. Rev. Stat. Ann. §8-4-104).

CONNECTICUT

If you are fired: next business day; if you quit: next scheduled payday (Conn. Gen. Stat. Ann. §1-71c).

DELAWARE

Next scheduled payday (Del. Code Ann. §19-1103).

DISTRICT OF COLUMBIA

If you are fired: next business day; if you quit: next scheduled payday or within seven days, whichever is sooner (D.C. Code §36-103).

HAWAII

If you are fired: next business day; if you quit: next scheduled payday (Hawaii Rev. Stat. §388-3).

IDAHO

Next scheduled payday or within ten business days, whichever is sooner. If written request is made for earlier payment, within forty-eight hours (Idaho Code §45-606).

ILLINOIS

Next scheduled payday (820 Ill. Cons. Stat. 115/5).

INDIANA

Next scheduled payday (Ind. Code §§22-2-9-2 and 22-2-5-1).

IOWA

Next scheduled payday (Iowa Code Ann. §91A.4).

KANSAS

Next scheduled payday (Kans. Stat. Ann. §31-315).

KENTUCKY

If you are fired: next scheduled payday or within fourteen days, whichever is later; if you quit: no applicable law (Ky. Rev. Stat. Ann. §337.055).

LOUISIANA

Within three days of your date of discharge or resignation (La. Rcv. Stat. Ann. §23-631).

MAINE

Next scheduled payday or within two weeks after demand, whichever is earlier (Maine Rev. Stat. Ann., t. 26, §626).

MARYLAND

Next scheduled payday (Md. Lab. & Empl. Code Ann. §3-505).

MASSACHUSETTS

If you are fired: immediately; if you quit: next scheduled payday (Mass. Ann. Laws, ch. 149, §148).

MICHIGAN

As soon as the amount can be determined with due diligence (Mich. Stat. Ann. §17.277(5)).

MINNESOTA

If you are fired: within twenty-four hours of demand; if you quit: within five days, or within twenty-four hours if you have given at least five days' notice (Minn. Stat. Ann. §§181.13 and 181.14).

MISSOURI

If you are fired: within seven days after you make a written demand; if you quit: no applicable law (Mo. Ann. Stat. §290.110).

MONTANA

If you are fired for cause: immediately; otherwise, within three days. An extension of three additional days is given to the employer if its payroll checks come from outside the state (Mont. Code. Ann. §39-3-205).

NEBRASKA

If you are fired: next scheduled payday or within two weeks, whichever is sooner; if you quit: no applicable law (Nebr. Rev. Stat. §48-1230).

NEVADA

If you are fired: immediately; if you quit: next scheduled payday or within seven days, whichever is earlier (Nev. Rev. Stat. §§608.020 and 608.030).

NEW HAMPSHIRE

If you are fired: within seventy-two hours; if you quit: next scheduled payday; of if you give at least one pay period's notice, within seventy-two hours of end of work. (N.H. Rev. Stat. Ann. §275:44).

NEW JERSEY

Next scheduled payday (N.J. Stat. Ann. §34:11-4.3).

NEW MEXICO

If you are fired: within five days; if you quit: no applicable law (N.Mex. Stat. Ann. §§50-4-4 and 50-4-5).

NEW YORK

If you are fired: next scheduled payday; if you quit: no applicable law (N.Y. Lab. Laws §191).

NORTH CAROLINA

Next scheduled payday (N.C. Gen. Stat. §95.25.7).

NORTH DAKOTA

If you are fired: within twenty-four hours of the time of separation at employer's place of business or within fifteen days or on the next scheduled payday, whichever comes first; if you resign: next scheduled payday by certified mail to an address designated by the employee (N.Dak. Cent. Code §34-14-03).

OKLAHOMA

Next scheduled payday (Okla. Stat. Ann., t. 40, §165.3).

OREGON

If you are fired: immediately; if you quit: within forty-eight hours (Oreg. Rev. Stat. §652.140).

PENNSYLVANIA

Next scheduled payday (Pa. Stat. Ann., t. 43, §260.5).

RHODE ISLAND

Next scheduled payday under normal circumstances; within twenty-four hours if the employer is going out of business, merging, or moving out of state (R.I. Gen. Laws §28-14-4).

SOUTH CAROLINA

Within forty-eight hours or on next scheduled payday, which may not be more than thirty days after written notice is given (S.C. Cod. Laws §41-11-170).

SOUTH DAKOTA

If you are fired: within five days after you have returned anything belonging to the employer; if you quit: next scheduled payday after you have returned anything belonging to the employer (S.Dak. Cod. Laws §§60-11-10 and 60-11-11).

TEXAS

If you are fired: within six days; if you quit: next regularly scheduled payday (Tex. Civ. Stat., art. 5155).

UTAH

If you are fired: within twenty-four hours; if you quit: within seventy-two hours, or immediately if you have given at least seventy-two hours' notice (Utah Code Ann. §34-28-5).

VERMONT

If you are fired: within seventy-two hours; if you quit: next scheduled payday or, if no scheduled payday exists, the next Friday (Vt. Stat. Ann., t. 21, §342).

VIRGINIA

Next scheduled payday (Va. Code §40.1-29).

WASHINGTON

Next scheduled payday (Wash. Rev. Code §49.48.010).

WEST VIRGINIA

If you are fired: within seventy-two hours; if you quit: next regular payday (W.Va. Code §21-5-4).

WISCONSIN

If you are fired: within three days; if you quit: within fifteen days (Wis. Stat. Ann. §109.03).

WYOMING

If you are fired: within twenty-four hours; if you quit: within seventy-two hours (Wyo. Stat. Ann. §27-4-103).

C. Sample Forms

EMPLOYEE
ACKNOWLEDGMENT

Please read the following information and return this acknowledgment form, dated and signed, to your direct supervisor for inclusion in your personnel file.

This handbook is provided to you for information and immediate reference. Because we are a dynamic and changing organization, policies included in this handbook are subject to change, revision, deletion, or addition by this organization from time to time with or without prior notice.

No policy in this handbook should be interpreted as in any way changing, altering, or nullifying our policy of voluntary, at-will employment. Your employment with this organization has no specified duration, and either you or the organization may terminate the employment relationship whenever either of us believes it is desirable to do so, without consideration of cause or notice. The at-will nature of our relationship may not be changed except by a separate written agreement specifically entered into for such purpose and signed by the board chair.

ACKNOWLEDGMENT

This is to acknowledge that I have received and read my copy of the handbook, am familiar with and understand its contents, and agree to comply with its terms during my employment.

(Please print)

Name: _____

Date: _____

Title: _____

Signature: _____

WRITTEN WARNING
DOCUMENT

1. Reason for the warning _____

_____

2. Description of the problem _____

_____

3. Impact on work, department, and organization, as applicable _____

_____

4. Supporting examples _____

_____

5. Desired improvement _____

_____

6. How progress will be monitored _____

_____

7. Consequences if improvement does not occur _____

_____

8. Supervisor signature and date _____

_____

9. Employee signature and date _____

Signature: _____

Date: _____

JOB DESCRIPTION

Title: Director of Operations
Reports to: Executive Director
Job Status: Exempt

POSITION SUMMARY

The Director of Operations is responsible for ensuring the delivery of administrative services to foundation donors, client foundations, and grantees in a manner that upholds the standards of excellence associated with the Foundation.

MAJOR RESPONSIBILITIES

- *Budgeting:* Develops, manages, and reviews budgets for all areas of responsibility to ensure the efficient provision of support and services.

- *Leadership and Teamwork:* Manages and develops a staff of administrative and support personnel. Creates and maintains a diverse, professional, results-oriented work environment that emphasizes teamwork and ensures respect and recognition for each employee's contribution to the Foundation's success. Works in partnership with other members of the senior management team to address all issues relating to the successful operation of the Foundation. Develops and maintains strong working partnerships with key "clients" within and outside of the Foundation.

- *Administrative Systems:* Designs, implements, monitors, and evaluates internal grantmaking systems including grants database, administrative services to client foundations, and proposal intake.

- *Reporting:* Designs, implements, monitors, and evaluates effective communications vehicles including grantee notifications, docket calendars, client reports, client evaluation and feedback documents, and intradepartmental communications.

- *Office Support:* Ensures quality of administrative support services for all members of the grants program staff.

- *Planning:* Functions as an active, effective member of the Foundation's senior management team. Participates in the development of annual and long-term strategic plans for all areas of the organization.

ORGANIZATIONAL RELATIONSHIPS

Has supervisory responsibility for and frequent contact with the administrative staff. Works in close partnership with the Executive Director, CFO, and Program Director. Has regular contact with Foundation staff in the finance and program areas. Has some contact with donors and grantees. Has some contact with the Board President, Vice President, and Director of Special Projects.

JOB DESCRIPTION, continued

QUALIFICATIONS

- *Experience:* This position requires a minimum of five years of administrative and management experience, preferably with a public or private foundation. Experience should emphasize the development of administrative, operations, or reporting systems in a service-driven environment. Supervisory experience is required.

- *Knowledge:* A solid foundation in general business and administrative practices is essential. A good basic knowledge of accounting fundamentals is required, as is a high degree of comfort working with computers and information systems as tools for managing processes and information. Understanding of the functions of a grantmaking organization is preferred.

- *Skills and Abilities:* A proven ability to manage complex systems and processes in a fast-paced, informal work environment is required. Outstanding interpersonal skills and the ability to relate well to diverse individuals at all organizational levels are also indispensable. A strong results orientation, openness to new ideas, and a proven ability to deliver a consistently high quality of service to both external clients and internal work partners is expected. Excellent written and verbal communications skills are required, as is an aptitude for managing multiple projects simultaneously. This position requires proven analytical skills and a fanatical attention to detail.

POSITION DESCRIPTION FORM

Position: _____

_____

Organization: _____

_____

Supervisor: _____

_____

Work Schedule: _____

_____

Status: _____

_____

Salary: _____

_____

Primary Function: _____

_____

Major Duties and Responsibilities: _____

_____

Organizational Relationships: _____

_____

Knowledge and Experience: _____

_____

Skills: _____

_____

_____

_____

_____

PERFORMANCE EVALUATION FORM

Employee Name: _____

Supervisor's Name: _____

Position: _____

Date of last review or hire date: _____ _____

This annual performance evaluation and development plan is meant to give both employee and supervisor a formal opportunity to review the accomplishments and milestones of the past twelve months, to identify areas of strength and areas for growth, and to develop a new set of goals for the coming year.

Steps

1. Employee completes a self-review, including an evaluation of goals achieved, accomplishments, and special projects, as well as a key skills evaluation. Employee reviews his or her job description and notes any significant changes in responsibilities over the past twelve months.

2. Supervisor receives the employee's self-review.

3. Supervisor evaluates the employee's job performance by reviewing the job description, evaluating goals achieved, accomplishments, and special projects, and completing a key skills evaluation. Appropriate changes are made to the job description.

4. Supervisor and employee meet for formal evaluation discussion. Supervisor and employee together set goals for coming year.

GOALS REVIEW

Current Evaluation Goals (review goals from last performance review): _____

_____

Job Performance Goals: _____

_____

Personal Development Goals: _____

_____

Accomplishments and Special Projects (note projects and assignments completed and any special projects undertaken during review period): _____

_____

_____

PERFORMANCE EVALUATION FORM, continued

GOALS FOR NEXT EVALUATION

Job Performance Goals

1. _____

_____

2. _____

_____

3. _____

_____

Personal Development Goals

1. _____

_____

2. _____

_____

Support to be Provided by Supervisor (including regularly scheduled check-ins)

_____   _____
Employee's Signature   Supervisor's Signature

_____   _____
Date   Date

D. The Management Center Human Resources Assistance

From recruitment and hiring to evaluation and compensation, The Management Center is Northern California's foremost provider of human resources assistance to nonprofits. In addition to publishing this handbook, we offer the following services:

HUMAN RESOURCES CONSULTING SERVICES

We've been helping good causes manage better since 1977 through professional consulting services. Our team of experienced consultants is available to help you with:

- Customizing *Creating Your Employee Handbook*
- Team building
- Performance management systems
- Compensation studies
- Board strategic planning
- Mediation
- Leadership management training

OPPORTUNITY NOCS

Launched in 1986, this weekly publication of nonprofit organization classifieds (NOCs) is Northern California's most comprehensive source of diverse employment opportunities in the fields of health, education, social services, the environment, and the arts. We have regional affiliates with publications in Atlanta, Boston, Dallas, Los Angeles, and Philadelphia, plus a new national *Opportunity NOCs* website at *http://www.opportunitynocs.org.*

TEMPEXECS

Created by The Management Center, TempExecs offers an interim management service to place seasoned professionals with nonprofit organizations.

EXECUTIVE SEARCH SERVICES

This program assists nonprofit organizations in conducting management searches. In addition to direct efforts, the program also utilizes consultants from the private business sector for executive searches.

WAGE & BENEFIT SURVEY

The only survey of its kind in Northern California, the *Wage & Benefit Survey* is a comprehensive report of current salaries and benefits paid to nonprofit personnel. Published by The Management Center since 1979, the *Survey* is an essential tool for determining nonprofit compensation levels.

COMPENSATION GUIDE

Written by Fred Kohler as a companion to this book and TMC's *Wage & Benefit Survey*, this guide provides direction on how to implement fair compensation systems and how to administer and maintain these systems.

HR SKILLBUILDERS

These popular workshops help participants develop performance management, hiring, and recruiting skills.

THE NONPROFIT ASSESSMENT TOOL

One of our highlighted on-line services is The Nonprofit Assessment Tool. This interactive questionnaire allows nonprofits to evaluate their organization's managerial performance in eight areas. Stop by our website at *http://www.tmcenter.org* to test-drive a module free of charge!

FOR MORE INFORMATION

Feel free to contact us for more information at:

The Management Center
870 Market Street, Suite 800
San Francisco, CA 94102-2903
Voice: (415) 362-9735
Fax: (415) 362-4603
E-mail: tmc@tmcenter.org
Internet: http://www.tmcenter.org

Index

A

Absenteeism, 138
Accessible workplace. *See* Americans with Disabilities Act (ADA)
Affirmative action, 17
Agency confidentiality, 153–154
AIDS/HIV nondiscrimination policy, 16, 137
Alcohol abuse. *See* Substance abuse policy
Americans with Disabilities Act (ADA), 18, 33, 195
Appearance and hygiene, 144
Arbitration, and employee termination, 171
"At will" employment, 2, 19, 181–182
Attendance and punctuality, 138
Automobiles, personal, business use of, 143

B

Benefit(s), 53–67; counseling and rehabilitation, 64, 101, 130–131; dependent care, 65, 66; disability, 60–61, 91–96; eligibility, 27, 32, 55–56; family and medical leave, 99; flexible spending accounts (FSAs), 63; paid time off, 71–87; personal use time, 65, 66; unpaid time off and leaves of absence, 89–106. *See also* Insurance
Bereavement leave, 86
Board members, employment of, 40
Break periods. *See* Meal and rest periods
By-the-Book Approach, in sample handbook, 6

C

Childbirth leave, 91, 93–94
Client confidentiality, 153–154

COBRA (Consolidated Omnibus Budget Reconciliation Act), 57, 186
Communication, internal, 156; and complaint procedures, 169–171; open-door policy of, 165
Compensation philosophy, 121
Compensatory time off, 117
Complaint procedures, 169–171
Computer usage, 149–150
Conduct: standards of, 161–176; unacceptable, and termination of employment, 185
Confidentiality: of agency and client information, 153–154; and disclosure of life-threatening illness, 137; and on-the-job visitors, 140; of personnel files, 152–153; of voice and electronic mail, 149
Conflict resolution, 164
Conflict-of-interest policy, 172–173
Contractors, dealings with, 176
Counseling services, 64
Creative Approach, in sample handbook, 5–6
Credit unions, 67

D

Dental insurance, 53
Dependent care benefits, 65, 66
Disability insurance, state-funded, 60–61
Disability leave: benefits, 94–95; eligibility, 95; legal aspects of, 91; and permanent/long-term impairment, 97; and reemployment, 92; and work-related illness/injury, 94
Disciplinary procedures, 166–168
Diverse workforce: and holidays, 74; and nondiscriminatory policies, 15–18
Domestic partners, defined, 55–56
Dress and cleanliness, 144

Drug abuse. *See* Substance abuse policy
Drug-free workplace, 129–131; state-by-state provisions, 205–208
Drug-Free Workplace Act, 129

E

Education and professional development, 46–47
Elder care provisions, 65
E-mail, confidentiality of, 149
Employee acknowledgment form, 240
Employee assistance programs (EAPs), 64
Employee classification, 29–31; change in, 32
Employee development policies, 43–47
Employee referral bonus programs, 37
Employee status, 29
Employee transfers and promotions, 35–36, 45
Equal employment opportunity (EEO) policy, 15–16; state-by-state provisions, 196–204
Exempt versus nonexempt status: guidelines, 29; and overtime, 117; timekeeping requirements for, 116
Exit interviews, 188
Expense reimbursement, 145

F

Facilities and property, use of, 139
Fair Labor Standards Act (FLSA), 29
Family: employment of, 38–39; immediate, defined, 55
Family and Medical Leave Act, 66
Family and medical leave policy, 91, 98–99; state-by-state provisions, 209–214
Fees and honoraria, 175

Reader Response Form

We'd like to receive your comments about *Creating Your Employee Handbook.* Your feedback will be incorporated into future editions. Please fill out the following form, making a photocopy first, and fax it to us at (415) 362-4603 or mail it to: The Management Center, 870 Market Street, Suite 800, San Francisco, CA 94102-2903.

1. Do you represent a nonprofit agency? ❑ yes ❑ no

2. How many staff members does your organization have? _____
   _____

3. What is your annual budget? _____

4. In general, which approach did you choose to follow?
   ❑ Creative Approach ❑ By-the-Book Approach
   ❑ Leading-Edge Approach

5. How did you use *Creating Your Employee Handbook*?
   ❑ To write a new personnel handbook
   ❑ To revise an existing personnel handbook
   ❑ As a general human resources tool
   ❑ In some other way (specify:_____)

6. How successfully did the author fulfill your needs?
   Any suggestions for improvements? _____
   _____

7. Is the content of the book accurate? Complete? _____
   _____

8. Is the book well organized? Clear? Easy to follow? Effective?
   _____

9. Is the book written in a clear, readable style? ❑ yes ❑ no

10. What other books on the topic have you read? How does this book
    differ? How is it better? Worse? _____
    _____

11. Overall, how would you rate this book? (please circle one choice)

    (low) 1 2 3 4 5 (high)

12. Additional comments: _____
    _____

How to Use This Disk

The minimum configuration needed to utilize the files included on this disk is a computer system with one 3.5" floppy disk drive capable of reading double-sided high-density IBM formatted floppy disks and word processing or desktop publishing software able to read Microsoft WORD 6.0/95 files. Document memory needs will vary, but your system should be capable of opening file sizes of 50 + K. No monitor requirements other than the ones established by your document software need be met.

Each of the policies and forms in your book has been saved onto the enclosed disk as a Microsoft WORD 6.0/95 file. These files can be opened with many Windows- and Macintosh-based word processors or desktop publishers for viewing or editing as you see fit. The files were originally created and saved as a WORD 6.0/95 DOC file by Microsoft Word 97. Not all software will read the files exactly the same, but the DOC format is an honest attempt by Jossey-Bass Publishers to preserve the composition of the figures such as borders, fonts, character attributes, bullets, etc. as accurately as possible.

Copy all DOC files to a directory/folder in your computer system. To read the files using your Windows-based document software, select File from the main menu followed by Open to display the Open dialog box. Set the correct drive letter and subdirectory shown in the Open dialog box by using the Look-in control. In the Files of Type text box enter *.doc to display the list of DOC files available in the subdirectory.

Each file name is coded to its material in the book to make it easy for you to find the text you want. For example, By-the-Book Agency material has been named BytheBook.DOC. You can open the file by either double-clicking your mouse on the file name that you want to open or by clicking once on the file name to select it and then once on the Open command button.